PROPORTIONAL MEASUREMENT ACUPUNCTURE

Acupuncture points are located relative to anatomical structures (landmarks) and by proportional measurement. The unit of proportional measurement is the Cun, and is measured as follows:

- 1 Cun is the *greatest width* of the thumb (1st phalanx).
- 2 Cun is the width of the middle, index and ring fingers (2/3/4 phalanx) together at their *most distal region*.
- 3 Cun is the middle, index, ring and little fingers (2/3/4/5 phalanx) together at the *widest area over the knuckles*.

fig 1.

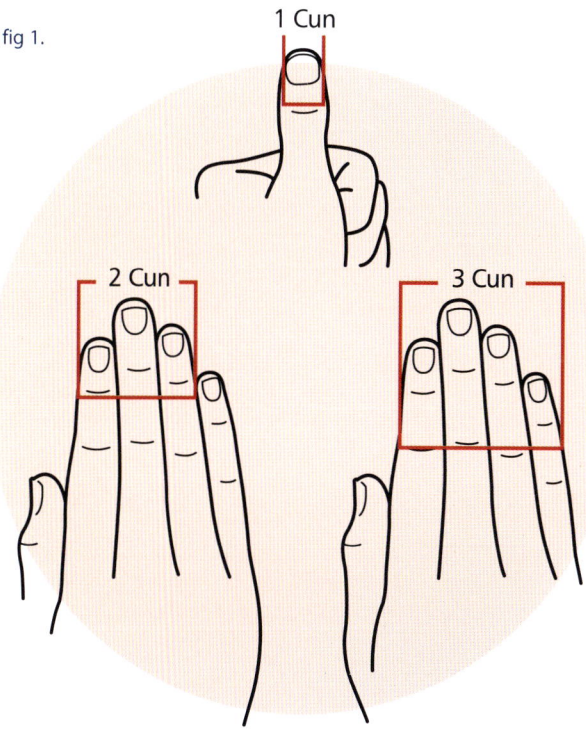

ACUPUNCTURE POINTS

LUNG (LU)

LUNG 1

Location: On the lateral side of the upper chest, within the first intercostal space. The point lies 6 cun lateral to the midline, and 1 cun inferior to LU- 2 which lies within the subclavicular fossa (fig 2).

Needling: Transverse-oblique insertion 0.5 laterally towards the coracoid process. Avoid deep needling as this runs the risk of piercing the lung.

Note: This point lies caudal to the subclavian artery. It is also slightly medial to the coracoid process.

Uses: (i) The proximity of this point to the coracoid process makes it a useful trigger point for the pectoralis minor muscle. This can be effectively treated using acupressure rather than needling however. (ii) Traditionally LU-1 is the *front Mu point* of the Lung and is used to *descend Lung Qi* to alleviate symptoms such as cough and wheezing.

LUNG 2

Location: 6 cun lateral to the anterior midline, the point lies below the clavicle within the delto-pectoral triangle (fig 2).

Needling: Oblique insertion 0.5-0.8 cun

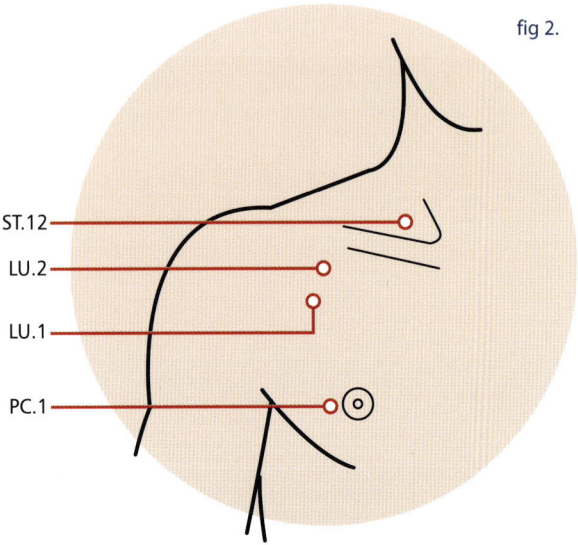

fig 2.

ACUPUNCTURE POINTS

Note: (i) Locate the delto-pectoral triangle by asking the patient to reach their arm forwards (flexion-abduction). (ii) This point lies 1 cun above and slightly medial to LU-1

Uses: (i) Local point for delto-pectoral pain (ii) traditionally used to *clear heat* and *descend Lung Qi*.

LUNG 3

Location: On the upper arm in the shallow depression between the humerus and biceps muscle. The point lies 3 cun inferior to the anterior axillary crease (fig 3).

Needling: Perpendicular or oblique insertion 0.5 to 1 cun.

Note: The distance between the anterior axillary crease and the elbow (cubital crease) is 9 cun. To find LU-3 divide this distance into three equal parts and the point lies at the junction of the upper 1/3rd and lower 2/3rd .

Uses: (i) Local point for biceps muscle strain. (ii) LU-3 is traditionally known as a *window of heaven point* used to treat rebellious Qi. It can be used firstly for Lung conditions such as cough and wheezing, and secondly for head conditions including insomnia, and dizziness.

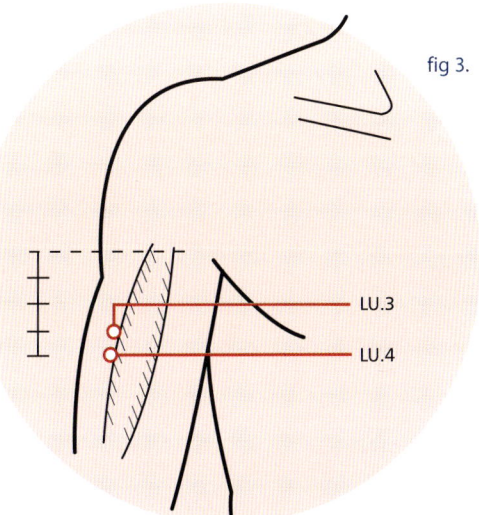

fig 3.

ACUPUNCTURE POINTS

LUNG 4

Location: On the upper arm in the shallow depression between the humerus and biceps muscle. The point lies 4 cun inferior to the anterior axillary crease, and 1 cun below LU-3 (fig 3).

Needling: Perpendicular or oblique insertion 0.5 to 1 cun.

Note: The distance between the anterior axillary crease and the elbow (cubital crease) is 9 cun. To find LU-4 divide this distance into three equal parts and the point lies 1 cun below the junction of the upper 1/3rd and lower 2/3rd.

Uses: (i) The proximity of LU-4 to the biceps makes it a useful local point for biceps muscle strain. (ii) LU-4 is traditionally used to *descend and regulate lung Qi* when treating chest conditions and chest tightness.

LUNG 5

Location: With the elbow slightly flexed, the point is located on the crease of the elbow, in the depression at the radial side (thumb side) of the biceps tendon (fig 4).

Needling: Perpendicular insertion 0.5 to 1 cun

Uses: (i) Used for biceps tendinopathy and movement restriction in the elbow. (ii) Traditionally used for coughing and breathing difficulties.

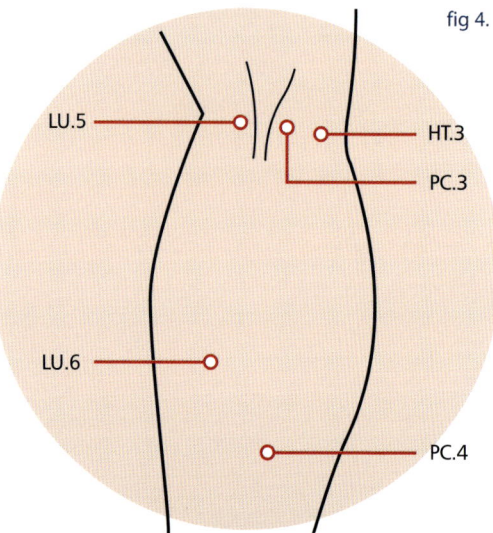

fig 4.

ACUPUNCTURE POINTS

LUNG 6

Location: On the flexor aspect of the forearm, on a line connecting point LU-5 (radial side of the biceps tendon at the elbow) with LU-9 (radial side of the wrist crease). The point lies 7 cun proximal to LU-9 (fig 4).

Needling: Perpendicular insertion 0.5 cun or oblique insertion 1.0 – 1.5 cun.

Note : LU-6 lies 1 cun proximal to the midpoint of the line joining Lu-5 and Lu-9.

Uses : (i) LU-6 can be a mid belly trigger point for the brachioradialis muscle. (ii) *Xi-cleft* point of the Lung channel (iii) Traditionally used to treat coughing and wheezing.

LUNG 7

Location: On the radial aspect of the forearm, proximal to the radial styloid, approximately 1.5 cun from the centre of the anatomical snuffbox (LI-5). The point lies in the cleft between the tendons of brachioradialis and abductor pollicis longus (fig 5).

Needling: Transverse insertion proximally 0.5 to 1 cun.

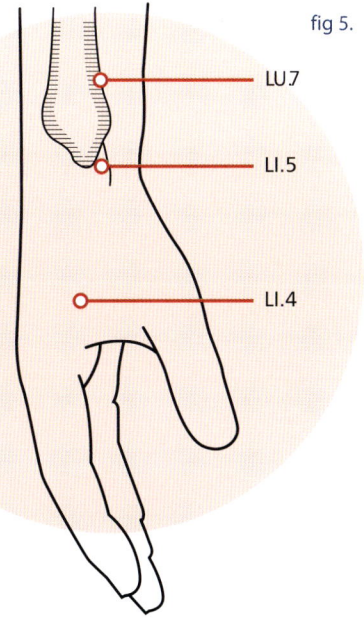

fig 5.

ACUPUNCTURE POINTS

LUNG 7 (CONT)

Note: (i) This point lies over the Cephalic vein (ii) Grip the styloid process between the thumb and second finger and run the index finger along the radius until it settles into a depression. This is made easier with the patients wrist in slight ulnar deviation.

Uses: (i) Used for local pain and thumb tendinopathy (De-Quervain's syndrome). (ii) *Command point* for pain in the neck and occiput. (iii) *Expels pathogenic wind* and *descends Lung Qi*. (iv) *Luo-connecting point* of the Lung channel and *Confluence point* for the Conception vessel.

LUNG 8

Location: On the palmar aspect of the wrist, 1 cun proximal to LU-9. The point lies in a shallow depression proximal to the radial styloid, on the ulnar side of the abductor pollicis longus tendon (fig 6).

Needling: Perpendicular or oblique insertion 0.3-0.5 cun

Note: This point lies close to the radial artery

Uses: (i) LU-8 may be used as a local point to treat tendinopathy of the abductor pollicis longus, and for pain relief following healed scaphoid fracture. (ii) Traditionally used to *descend Lung Qi* when treating cough or breathlessness.

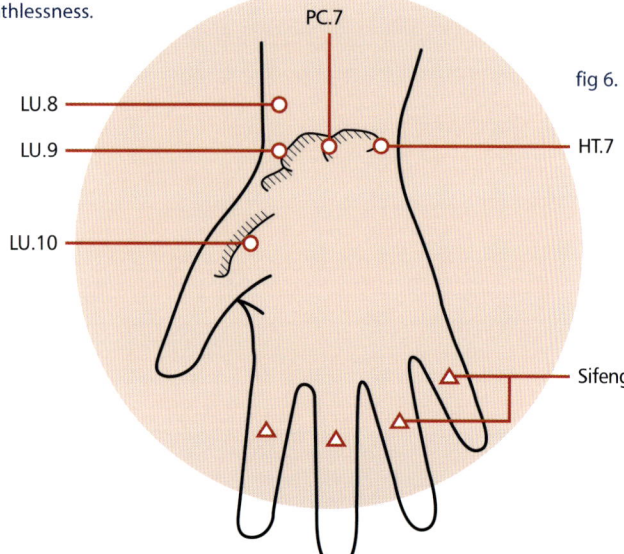

fig 6.

ACUPUNCTURE POINTS

LUNG 9

Location: At the radial end of the wrist joint crease. In the depression between the radial artery and the tendon of abductor pollicis longus. This point is level with HT-7 which is positioned in line with the pisiform bone (fig 7).

Needling: Perpendicular insertion 0.3 -0.5cun

Note: The point lies close to the radial artery, and the needle may pulse when in position.

Uses: (i) Local point for thumb and wrist pain. (ii) *Source point* of the lung channel to be used with any lung condition. (iii) *Influential point* for the vascular system.

LUNG 10

Location: On the thenar eminence of the hand, in the depression distal to the 1st metacarpophalangeal (MCP) joint. At the midpoint of the shaft of the first metacarpal bone (fig 7).

Needling: Perpendicular insertion 0.5 to 1 cun

Note: The point lies in a small hollow between the metacarpal shaft and the thenar eminence. It is traditionally said to lie at the junction of the red and white skin.

Uses: Local point for pain in the thumb joint.

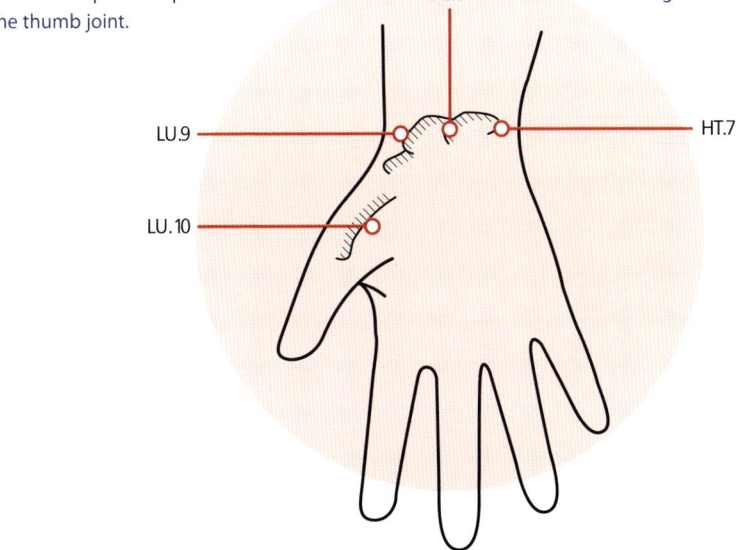

fig 7.

ACUPUNCTURE POINTS

LUNG 11

Location: Radial nail point of the thumb (fig 8).

Needling: Perpendicular 0.1 cun

Uses: Traditionally said to benefit the throat

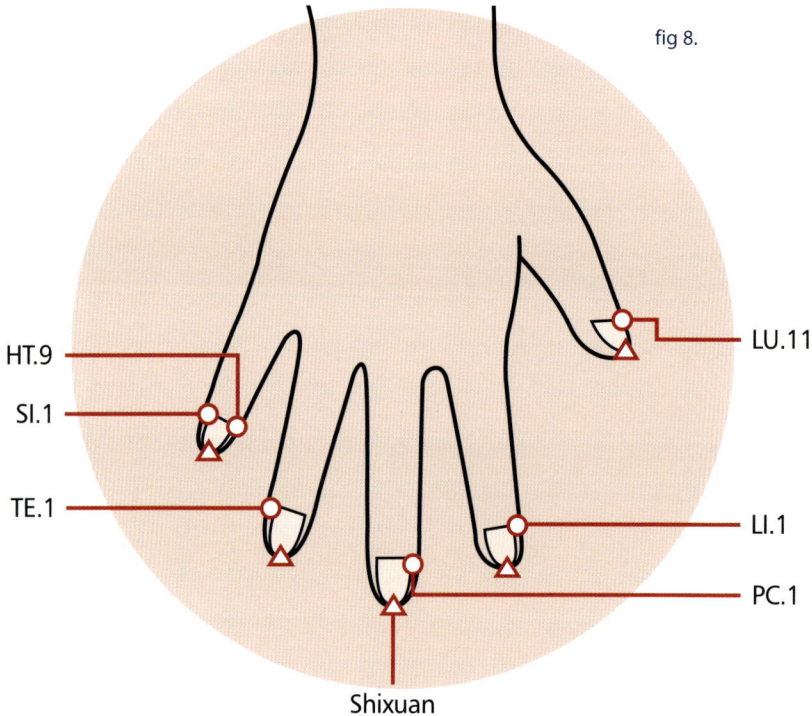

fig 8.

ACUPUNCTURE POINTS

LARGE INTESTINE (LI)

LARGE INTESTINE 1

Location: At the radial nail point of the index finger (2nd phalanx) (fig 9).

Needling: 0.1 cun perpendicular

Uses: Traditionally said to treat pain and inflammation of the throat and mouth.

LARGE INTESTINE 2

Location: On the radial border of the index finger, in a depression just distal to the side of the metacarpo-phalangeal (MCP) joint (fig 9).

Needling: Oblique or perpendicular insertion 0.2 to 0.3 cun.

Note: Locate and needle with the finger relaxed.

Uses: (i) Local point for pain in the MCP joint (ii) Used as an alternative to LI-1 to treat conditions of the upper channel such as tooth, mouth and eye symptoms.

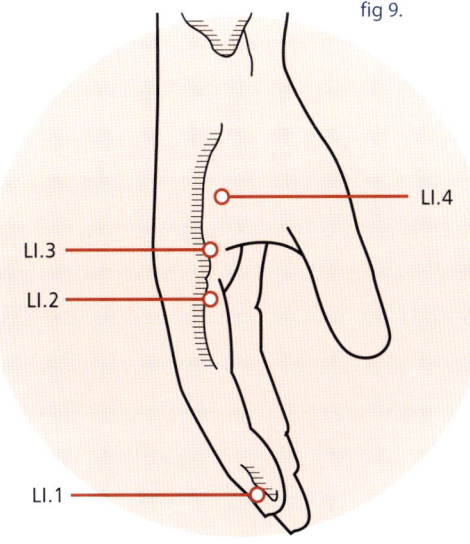

fig 9.

ACUPUNCTURE POINTS

LARGE INTESTINE 3

Location: On the radial side of the index finger, in the depression proximal to the head of the second metacarpal (fig 10).

Needling: Perpendicular or oblique insertion 0.3 - 0.5

Note: This point is easier to palpate and needle when the patient forms a loose fist.

Uses: (i) Local point for MCP joint pain. (ii) Traditionally used to treat symptoms in the *upper channel* (ear, nose, throat).

fig 10.

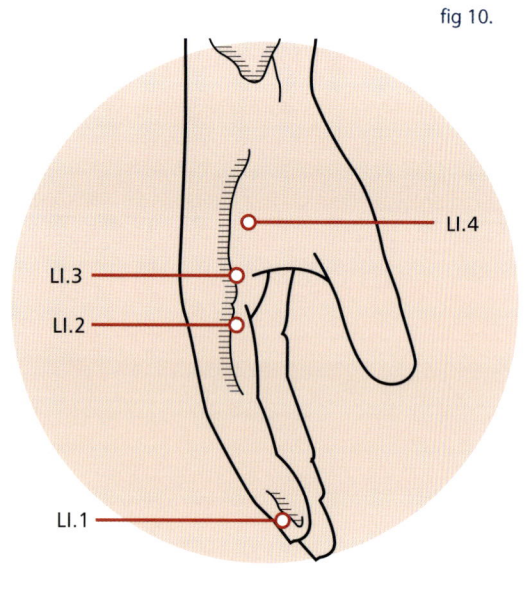

ACUPUNCTURE POINTS

LARGE INTESTINE 4

Location: On the dorsum of the hand, between the first and second metacarpal bones, within the adductor pollicis muscle. The point is at the midpoint of the second metacarpal bone, close to its radial border (fig 11).

Needling: Perpendicular insertion 0.5 to 1 cun. Caution: strong manipulation of this point can be contraindicated in pregnancy as it is traditionally said to promote childbirth.

Note: (i) the point lies on a line bisecting the angle formed by the 1st and 2nd metacarpals when the thumb is fully abducted (ii) when the thumb is fully adducted, the point lies at the highest point of the muscle bulge (dorsal interosseous muscle), (iii) the therapist places the distal phalanx of their own thumb onto the patients thumb web and points their thumb towards the patients metacarpal shaft. The point lies at the tip of the therapists thumb.

Uses: (i) Used for head and neck symptoms, headache and facial pain. (ii) One of the most widely used acupuncture points, LI-4 is a *heavenly star* point. (iii) *Source point* of the large intestine channel, and *command point* for the face and mouth.

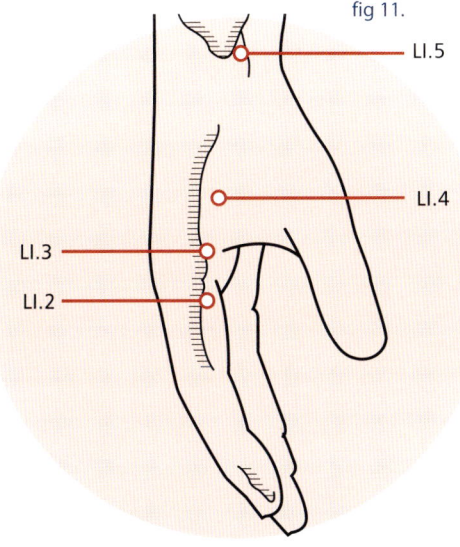

fig 11.

ACUPUNCTURE POINTS

LARGE INTESTINE 5

Location: On the radial side of the wrist, in the centre of the hollow formed between the tendons of extensor pollicis longus and extensor pollicis brevis (anatomical snuffbox) (fig 12).

Needling: Perpendicular insertion 0.3 - 0.5 cun

Note: (i) avoid needling directly into the cephalic vein which is usually clearly visible. (ii) Deep needling runs the risk of puncturing the dorsal carpal branch of the radial artery.

Uses: (i) Local point for radial wrist pain. (ii) Used to treat ENT symptoms including tinnitus. .

LARGE INTESTINE 6

Location: On a line connecting LI-5 with LI-11 the point lies 3 cun proximal to LI-5 (fig 12).

Needling: Oblique insertion 0.5- 1 cun

Note: Divide the line linking LI-5 to LI-11 (12 cun) into half (6 cun), and then divide the lower half again (3 cun). LI-6 lies at the distal quarter of the full line.

Uses: (i) Local point for pain in the radial aspect of the forearm. (ii) Traditionally used for deafness, tinnitus, and tooth conditions. (iii) *Luo-connecting point* of the Large Intestine channel.

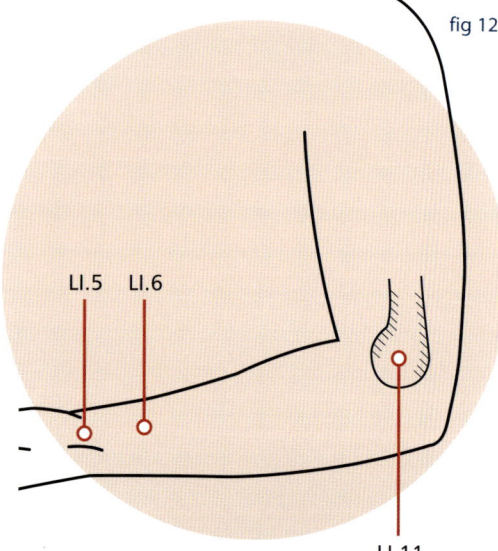

fig 12.

ACUPUNCTURE POINTS

LARGE INTESTINE 7

Location: On a line connecting LI-5 with LI-11 the point lies 5 cun proximal to LI-5 (fig 13)

Needling: Oblique insertion 0.5- 1 cun

Note: Divide the line linking LI-5 to LI-11 (12 cun) into half (6 cun), and LI-7 lies 1 cun distal to the mid point of the full line.

Uses: (i) Local point for pain in the radial aspect of the forearm. (ii) *Xi-cleft* point of the Large Intestine channel and as such used for acute conditions, in this case those affecting the head and abdomen.

LARGE INTESTINE 8 / 9 / 10

Location: On the radial side of the forearm, on a line connecting LI.-11 and LI.-5.
- LI-8 lies 4 cun distal to LI-11 (lateral elbow crease)(fig 13).
- LI-9 lies 3 cun distal to LI-11
- LI-10 lies 2 cun distal to LI-11

Needling: Perpendicular or oblique insertion 0.5 to 1.0 cun

Uses: (i) Local points for pain in the forearm including 'tennis elbow'. (ii) Trigger points for the extensor carpi radialis muscle (iii) traditionally used to *clear heat* and *expel pathogenic wind.*

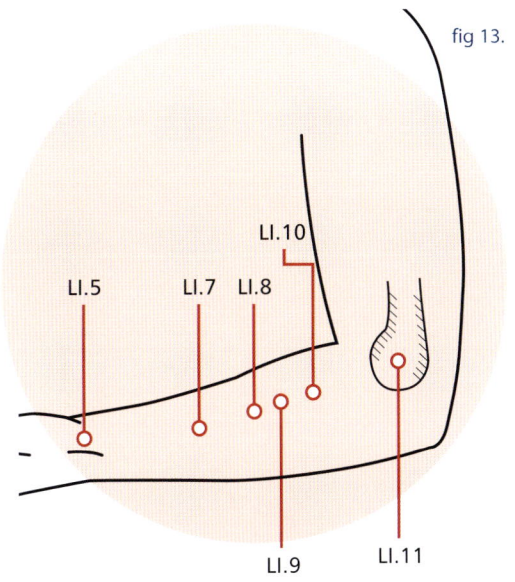

fig 13.

ACUPUNCTURE POINTS

LARGE INTESTINE 11

Location: With the elbow flexed, the point is midway between the radial aspect of the biceps tendon (LU 5) and the lateral epicondyle of the humerus. If the elbow is maximally flexed the point lies at the lateral end of the transverse cubital crease, within the belly of the extensor carpi radialis muscle (fig 14).

Needling: Perpendicular insertion 1 to 1.5 cun.

Note: Where there is marked tissue bulk two elbow creases may be apparent. Draw the skin proximally to reveal the cubital crease resulting from joint position alone. Use this crease for point location.

Uses: (i) Local point for pain in the elbow and lower arm including 'tennis elbow'. (ii) *Heavenly star* point traditionally used to *drain heat*. (iii) Often used to treat skin disorders.

LARGE INTESTINE 12

Location: 1 cun proximal to LI-11 at the lateral / posterior edge of the humerus (fig 14).

Needling: Perpendicular insertion 0.5 – 1.0 cun

Uses: Local point for elbow pain spreading up to the supracondylar ridge from the extensor carpi radialis longus muscle.

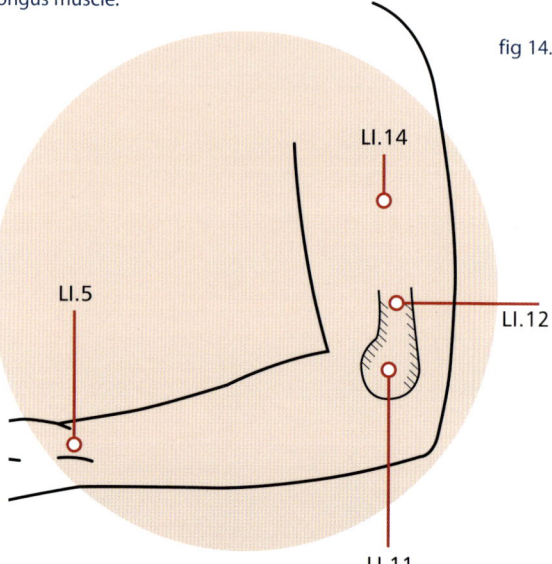

fig 14.

2nd Edition

ACUPUNCTURE POCKETBOOK

POINT LOCATION

Christopher M. Norris PhD MSc MCSP MBAcC

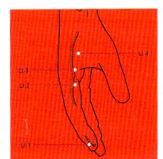 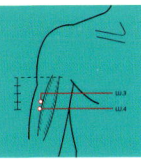 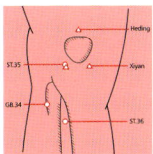 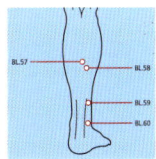

ACUPUNCTURE POCKETBOOK
Christopher Norris MSc MCSP CAc

CONTENTS

PROPORTIONAL MEASUREMENT IN ACUPUNCTURE	4
ACUPUNCTURE POINTS	5 - 188
• LUNG (LU)	5
• LARGE INTESTINE (LI)	12
• STOMACH (ST)	25
• SPLEEN (SP)	48
• HEART (HT)	59
• SMALL INTESTINE (SI)	66
• BLADDER (BL)	77
• KIDNEY (KI)	100
• PERICARDIUM (PC)	107
• TRIPLE ENERGISER (TE)	114
• GALL BLADDER (GB)	129
• LIVER (LR)	150
• GOVERNING VESSEL (GV)	160
• CONCEPTION VESSEL (CV)	168
EXTRA POINTS	
• UPPER EXTREMITY	174
• LOWER EXTREMITY	180
• HEAD AND NECK	182
• BACK	187
REFERENCES AND SOURCE MATERIAL	189
APPENDIX	190

ACUPUNCTURE POINTS

LARGE INTESTINE 13

Location: On the lateral side of the upper arm, 3 cun proximal to Ll.-11, on a line connecting Ll.-11 with Ll.-15 at the shoulder (fig 15).

Needling: Perpendicular insertion to 0.5 – 0.8 cun

Note: (i) The point lies in the depression between the biceps muscle and the humerus. (ii) Divide the line joining the anterior axillary fold and Ll-11 into three. Ll-13 lies at the junction of the lower 3rd of the full line

Uses: Pain in the upper arm.

LARGE INTESTINE 14

Location: On the lateral side of the upper arm, at the distal insertion of the deltoid muscle. The point lies approximately 2 cun caudal to the anterior axillary fold (fig 15).

Needling: 0.5 cun perpendicular or up to 1.5 cun using an oblique insertion.

Note: Use an isometric contraction of the Deltoid (abduct against resistance) to locate the muscle insertion.

Uses: Pain radiating from the shoulder into the elbow.

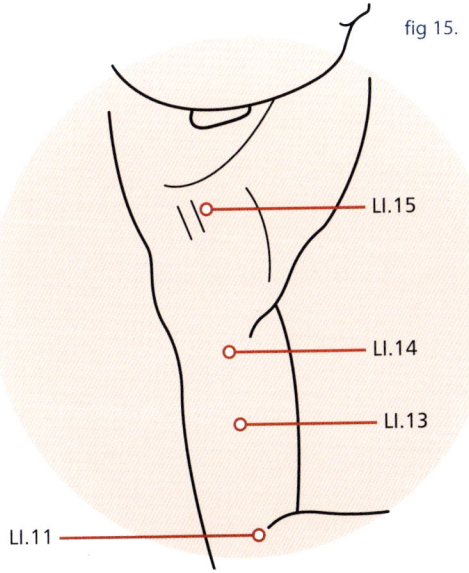

fig 15.

ACUPUNCTURE POINTS

LARGE INTESTINE 15

Location: In the depression anterior and inferior to the Acromion process, between the middle and anterior fibres of the deltoid muscle (fig 16).

Needling: With the arm abducted, use a perpendicular insertion directed towards the centre of the axilla, 1 – 1.5 cun. With the arm in a neutral position, use an oblique insertion directed distally 0.5 cun.

Note: (i) When the arm is abducted to 90°, the head of the humerus is drawn beneath the acromion process forming two sulci. LI-15 lies in the anterior sulcus (TE-14 in the posterior). (ii) Traditionally said to be the upper limb equivalent of ST-31 and used as a *gate point* to the limb.

Uses: (i) Pain and restricted movement in the shoulder (ii) *Meeting point* of the Large Intestine and Yang motility channels.

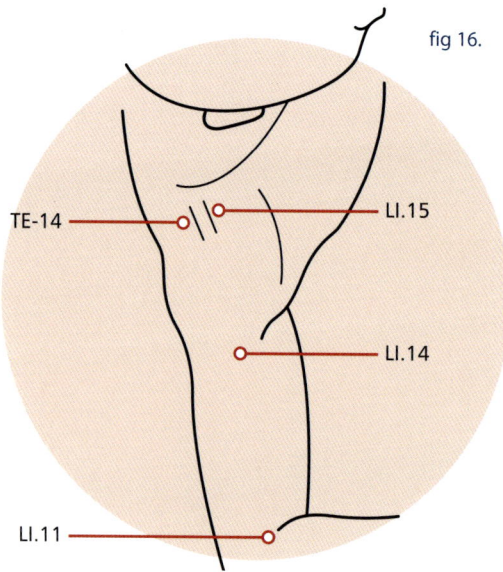

fig 16.

ACUPUNCTURE POINTS

LARGE INTESTINE 16

Location: In the depression between the lateral edge of the clavicle and the scapular spine, on the inner (medial) aspect of the acromion process (fig 17)

Needling: Perpendicular insertion 0.4 cun or oblique insertion directed laterally 0.6 cun.

Note: Deep medial insertion can puncture the lung causing a pneumothorax, in thin patients. This point lies close to the musculotendinous junction of the Supraspinatus muscle.

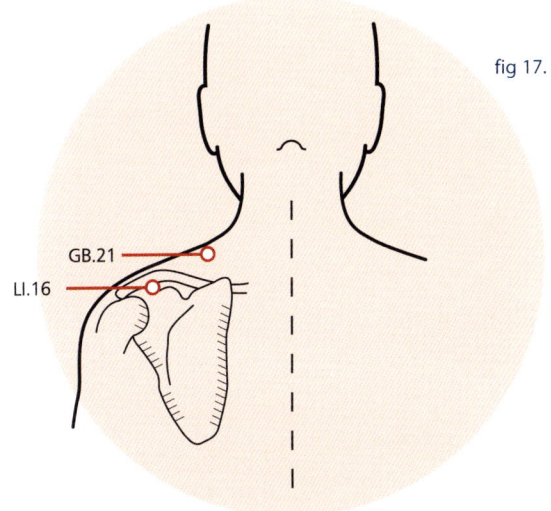

fig 17.

ACUPUNCTURE POINTS

LARGE INTESTINE 17

Location: On the lateral aspect of the neck at the posterior border of the sternocleido-mastoid muscle. The point lies 1 cun inferior and slightly posterior to LI-18 (fig 18)

Needling: Oblique or perpendicular insertion 0.3 to 0.5 cun.

Note: Deeper needling may puncture the carotid artery or jugular vein

Uses: Pain of the pharynx and throat. Local point for sternomastoid pain.

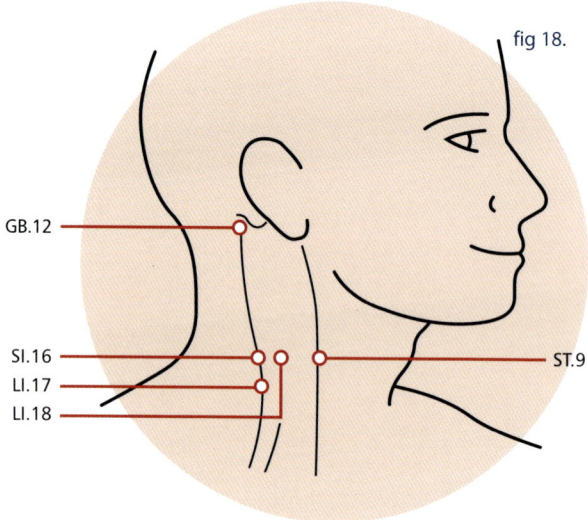

fig 18.

ACUPUNCTURE POINTS

LARGE INTESTINE 18

Location: On the lateral side of the neck, approximately 3 cun lateral to the tip of the Adam's apple (laryngeal prominence). Between the sternal and clavicular heads of the sternocleidomastoid muscle (fig 19).

Needling: Oblique or perpendicular insertion 0.3 to 0.5 cun.

Note: (i) Deeper needling may puncture the carotid artery or jugular vein (ii) Three points lie on a line level with the laryngeal prominence, LI-18, SI-16, and ST-9.

Uses: (i) Local point for sternomastoid pain. (ii) Pain of the pharynx and throat.

fig 19.

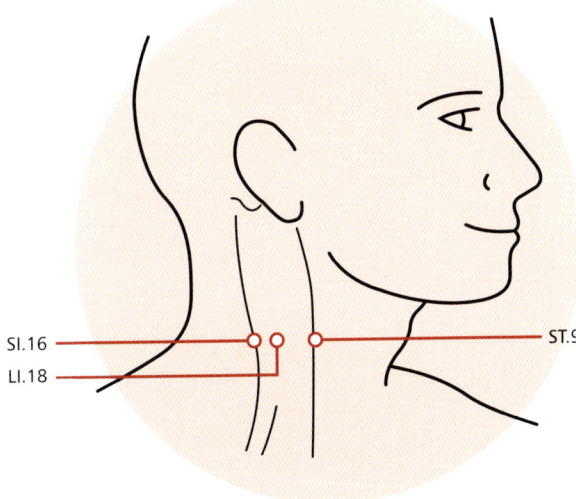

ACUPUNCTURE POINTS

LARGE INTESTINE 19

Location: On the upper lip 0.5 cun lateral to GV-26 (fig 20)

Needling: Oblique insertion 0.3-0.5 cun

Note: Skin should be swabbed before treatment, and needling should not be carried out through infected skin such as spots or acne.

Uses: Traditionally used to open the nasal passages, and to treat excessive nosebleeds (epistaxis).

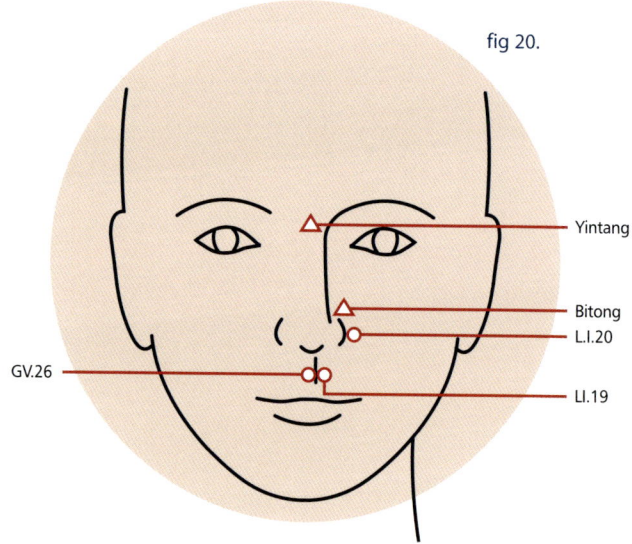

fig 20.

ACUPUNCTURE POINTS

LARGE INTESTINE 20

Location: In the naso-labial groove, level with the midpoint of the nostril (ala nasi) (fig 21).

Needling: Perpendicular insertion 0.2 cun or oblique insertion 0.5 cun.

Note: A branch of the facial vein passes close to this point and through it there is a risk of infection and thrombosis. Sterility is vital, skin should be swabbed well before treatment, and needling should not be carried out through infected skin such as spots or acne.

Uses: Congestion / discharge of the nose. Facial paralysis..

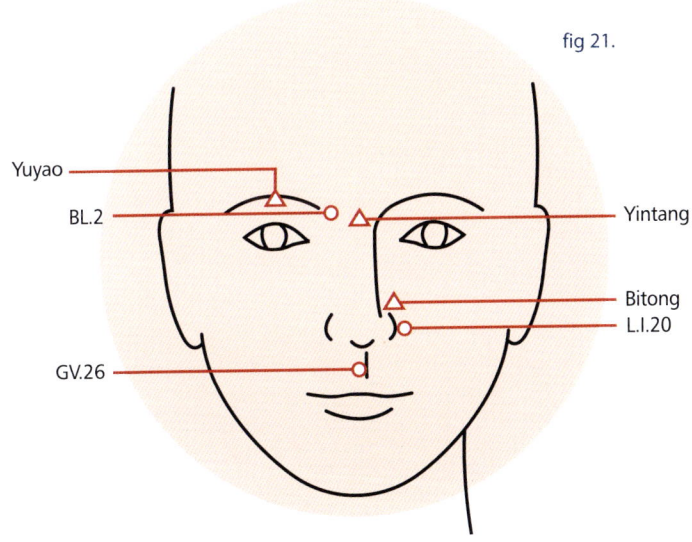

fig 21.

ACUPUNCTURE POINTS

STOMACH (ST)

STOMACH 1

Location: Directly below the pupil between the eyeball and the infraorbital foramen, with the patient looking forwards (fig 22).

Needling: 0.3 – 0.5 cun perpendicular insertion

Note: The patient should look upwards and close their eyes. The therapist gently presses upwards on the eyeball and inserts the needle, angling it slightly inferiorly.

Uses: Traditionally used to sharpen eyesight.

STOMACH 2

Location: In the depression of the infraorbital foramen, 1 cun directly below the pupil with the patient looking forwards (fig 22).

Needling: Perpendicular insertion 0.2 to 0.3 cun.

Uses: (i) Clinically more often used than ST-1 to sharpen eyesight. (ii) Also used for facial paralysis.

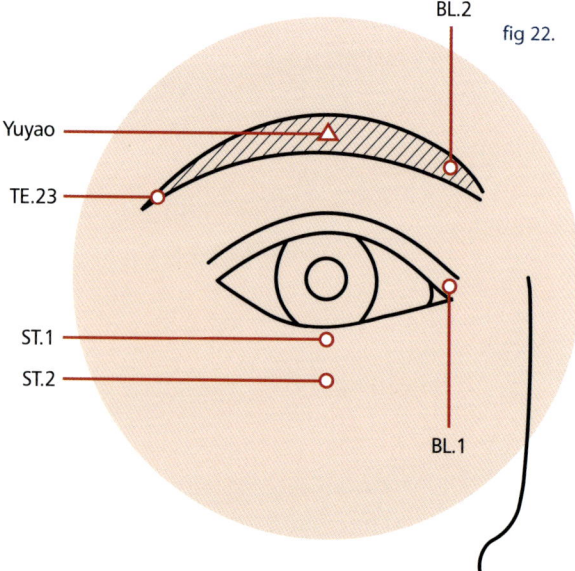

fig 22.

ACUPUNCTURE POINTS

STOMACH 3

Location: On the lower cheek at the junction of a vertical line drawn down from the pupil and a horizontal line drawn across from the base of the nose ((fig 23).

Needling: Perpendicular or oblique insertion 0.3 – 0.4 cun

Uses: (i) Local point for pain in the cheek and upper teeth. (ii) Traditionally used for deviation of the mouth.

STOMACH 4

Location: 0.4 cun lateral to the corner of the mouth (fig 23).

Needling: Perpendicular insertion 0.4 cun.

Uses: (i) Facial pain and paralysis, especially with deviation of the mouth. (ii) Often used for twitching of the facial muscles.

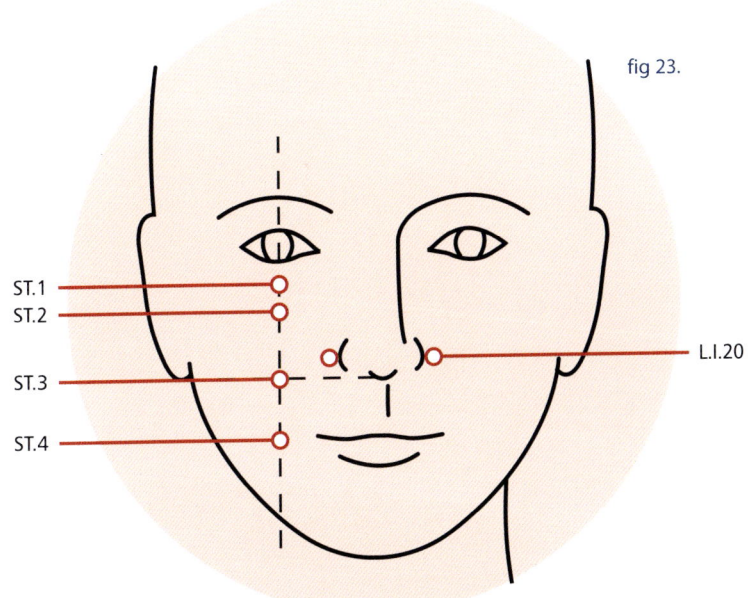

fig 23.

ACUPUNCTURE POINTS

STOMACH 5

Location: Directly anterior to the angle of the jaw, in a depression at the anterior border of the masseter muscle (fig 24).

Needling: Perpendicular insertion 0.3 to 0.5 cun.

Note: This point lies above the facial artery which should be located prior to needling. Use needle manipulation with caution.

Uses: (i) Toothache of the lower jaw. (ii) Inflammation of the salivary gland.

STOMACH 6

Location: One finger width anterior and superior to the angle of the jaw (fig 24).

Needling: Perpendicular insertion 0.3 - 0.5 cun.

Note: This point lies at the apex of the masseter muscle, when the patient bites firmly.

Uses: (i) ST-6 is a trigger point of the masseter muscle. (ii) May also be used for facial paralysis and pain / swelling of the teeth and face.

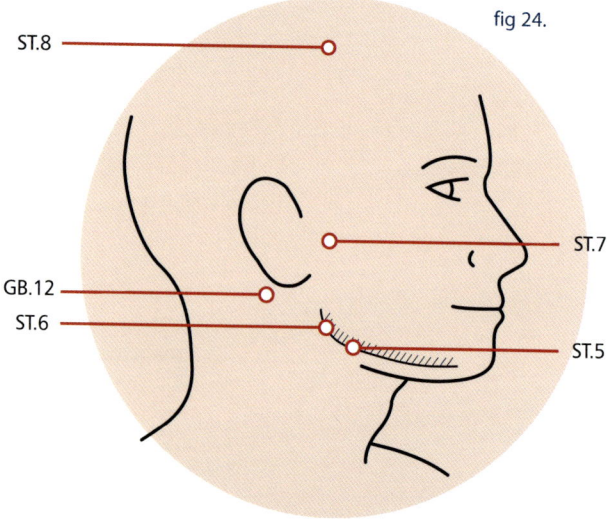

fig 24.

ACUPUNCTURE POINTS

STOMACH 7

Location: With the mouth closed, the point lies in the depression anterior to the condyloid process of the mandible, at the lower border of the zygomatic arch (fig 25).

Needling: Perpendicular insertion slightly inferiorly 0.5 cun.

Note: Palpation of the condyloid process is made easier with the mouth open. Once the process has been located, have the patient close their mouth and slide the palpating finger into the depression.

Uses: (i) Trigger point of the lateral pterygoid muscle. (ii) Used to treat toothache of the upper jaw, and pain in the temporomandibular joint (TMJ).

STOMACH 8

Location: At the temple 4.5 cun lateral to the midline and 0.5 cun within the anterior hairline (fig 25).

Needling: Transverse subcutaneous insertion 0.5 cun.

Note: (i) Where the hairline is no longer visible, ask the patient to frown to identify the frontal folds. (ii) This point lies close to the superficial temporal artery

Uses: (i) Trigger point of the temporalis muscle.
(ii) One sided headache focused over the eye.

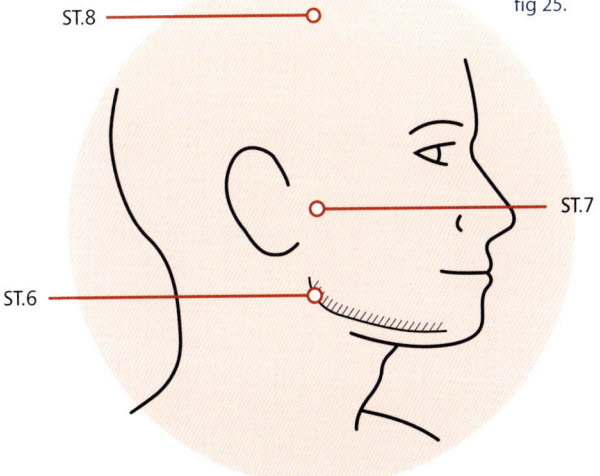

fig 25.

ACUPUNCTURE POINTS

STOMACH 9

Location: 1.5 cun lateral to the apex of the Adam's apple (laryngeal prominence), at the anterior edge of the sternocleidomastoid (SCM) muscle (fig 26)
Needling: Perpendicular or Oblique insertion 0.3 to 0.5 cun

Note: (i) This point is level with LI-18 which lies between the sternal and clavicular heads of the SCM, and SI-16 which lies on the posterior border of the SCM. The three points form a horizontal line across the bellies of SCM. (ii) the Carotid artery lies deep to this point.

Uses: Local point for neck and throat pain.

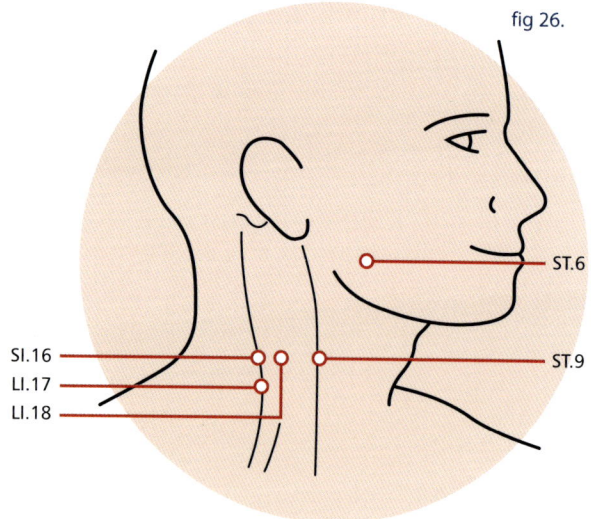

fig 26.

ACUPUNCTURE POINTS

STOMACH 11

Location: Just above the medial aspect of the clavicle, in a small depression between the sternal and clavicular heads of the sternocleidomastoid muscle (fig 27).

Needling: Perpendicular or oblique 0.3-0.5 cun

Note: (i) Ask the patient to rotate the head against resistance away from the side to be needled to make the muscle bellies stand out. (ii) the apex of the lung extends above the clavicle and so lies beneath this point.

Uses: (i) Local neck and throat pain. (ii) Traditionally used for *rebellious Qi* in cases of cough and hiccups.

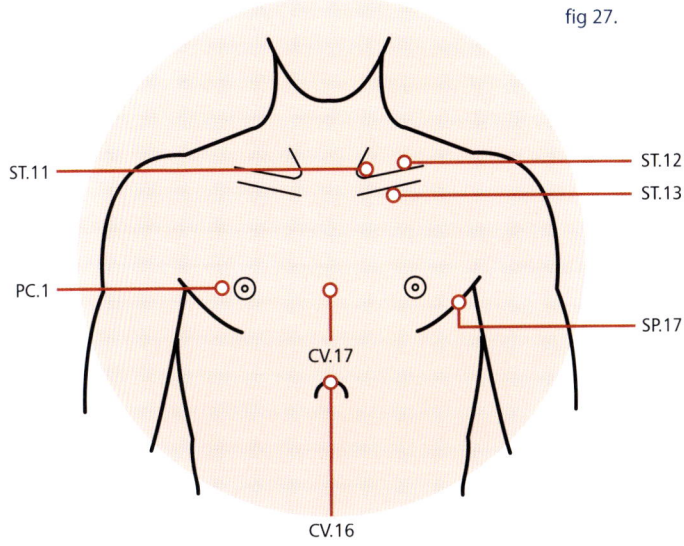

fig 27.

ACUPUNCTURE POINTS

STOMACH 12

Location: At the midpoint of the supraclavicular fossa, 4 cun lateral to the midline. The point lies on the superior border of the clavicle (fig 28).

Needling: 0.2 – 0.4 cun perpendicular, staying close to the clavicle.

Note: Deep needling and / or needling away from the posterior border of the clavicle may cause injury to the subclavian vessels or apex of the lung.

Uses: Cough, pain from the neck referred into the supraclavicular region.

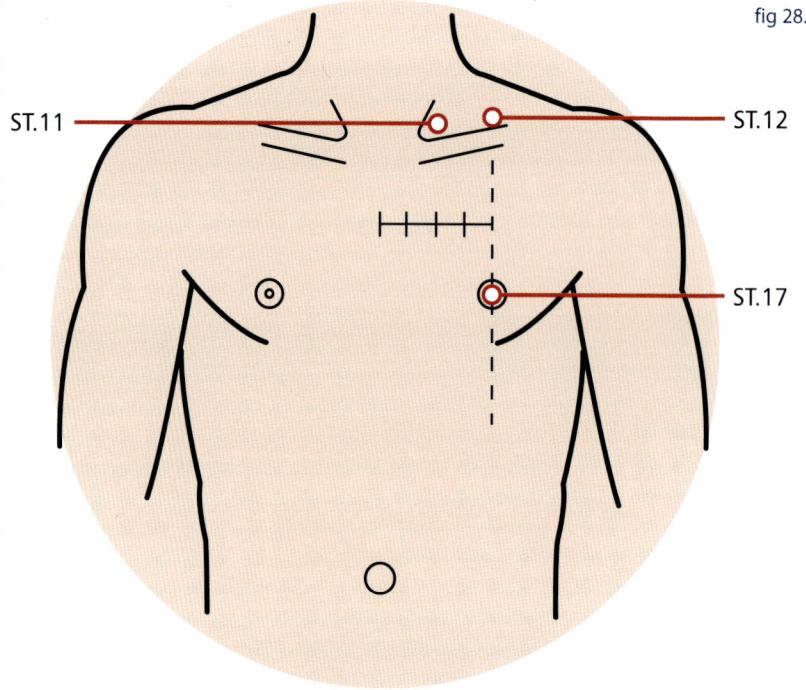

fig 28.

ACUPUNCTURE POINTS

STOMACH 13

Location: Directly below ST-12 on the inferior border of the clavicle, 4 cun lateral to the midline (fig 29).

Needling: Transverse or oblique needling 0.5 – 0.8 cun

Note: Deep needling may cause injury to the subclavian vessels or the apex of the lung.

Uses: Traditionally said to descend *rebellious Qi*, used for tightness in the chest, wheezing and cough.

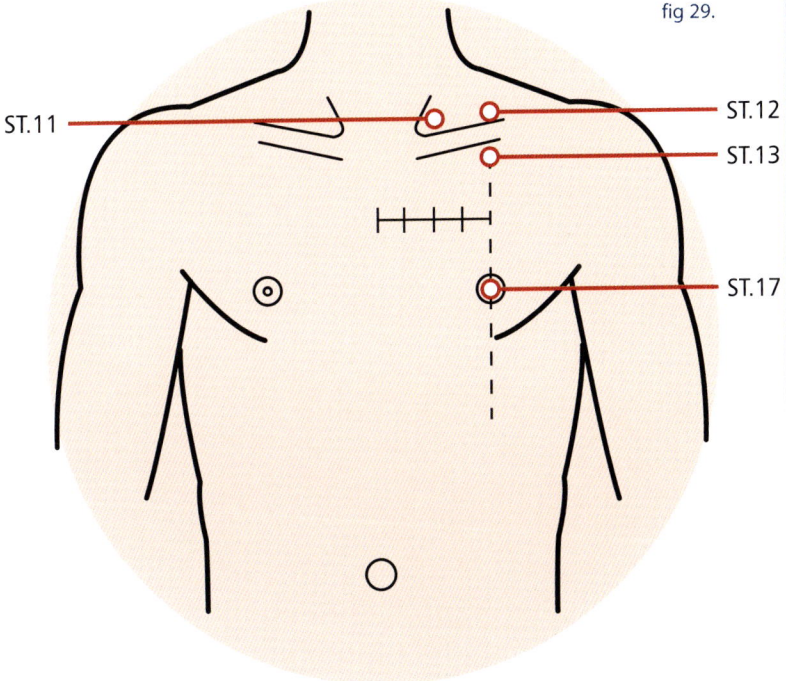

fig 29.

ACUPUNCTURE POINTS

STOMACH 14 / 15 / 16

Location: On the mamillary line 4 cun lateral to the midline (fig 30)
- ST 14 lies in the 1st intercostal space
- ST-15 lies in the 2nd intercostal space
- ST-16 lies in the 3rd intercostal space.

Needling: Transverse or oblique insertion along the length of the intercostals space 0.3 cun

Note: Deep needling risks pneumothorax

Uses: (i) local points for intercostal pain. (ii) Traditionally said to *unbind the chest* and *descend rebellious Qi* in the case of cough and dyspnoea.

STOMACH 17

Location: The nipple, which lies 4 cun lateral to the midline, over the 4th intercostal space (fig 30).

Needling: None
Note: In males the nipple lies in the 4th intercostal space

Uses: Location only

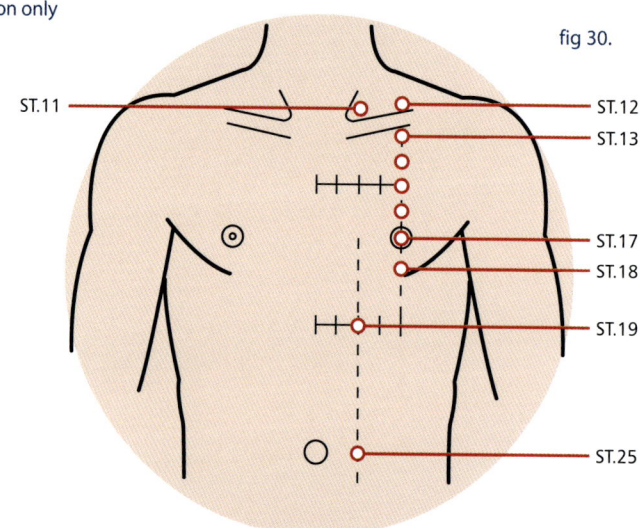

fig 30.

ACUPUNCTURE POINTS

STOMACH 18

Location: Directly below the nipple (ST-17) within the 5th intercostal space (fig 30).

Needling: Transverse subcutaneous insertion along the intercostal space 0.5 – 0.8 cun.

Uses: (i) Conditions of the breast such as insufficient lactation, soreness, abscess. (ii) Also used for cough and dyspnoea.

STOMACH 19 / 20 / 21 / 22 / 23 / 24

Location: Each point lies on the abdomen 2 cun lateral to the midline (centre of the umbilicus) (fig 31).
- ST 19 lies 6 cun superior to the umbilicus
- ST-20 lies 5 cun superior to the umbilicus
- ST-21 lies 4 cun superior to the umbilicus
- ST-22 lies 3 cun superior to the umbilicus
- ST-24 lies 1 cun superior to the umbilicus

Needling: Oblique or perpendicular insertion 0.5 -1.5 cun Needle depth being greater for lower points.

Note: (i) Deep needling may penetrate the peritoneum (ii) ST-19 lies on a horizontal line 2 cun below the sternocostal angle. (iii) ST-21 is level with the midpoint of a line connecting the umbilicus (CV-8) and the sternocostal angle (CV-16) (fig 31).

Uses: Traditionally used to *regulate Qi*, and as local points to relieve epigastric pain and abdominal distension.

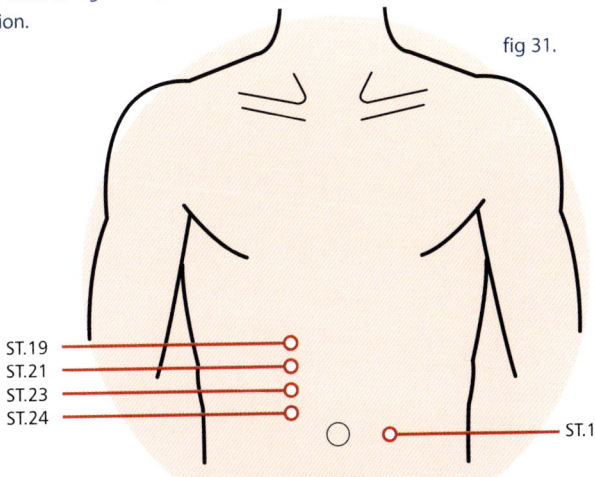

fig 31.

ACUPUNCTURE POINTS

STOMACH 25

Location: On the lower abdomen, 2 cun lateral to the umbilicus (fig 32).

Needling: Perpendicular or oblique insertion 1 to 1.5 cun.

Note: Use all lower abdominal points with caution in pregnancy

Uses: (i) Dysfunction of the intestines including diarrhoea and constipation, menstrual disorders, lower abdominal pain (ii) *Front Mu point* of the Large Intestine.

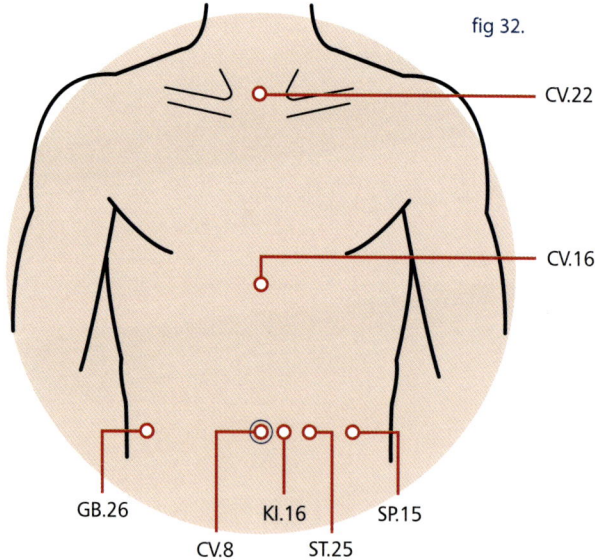

fig 32.

ACUPUNCTURE POINTS

STOMACH 26 / 27 / 28 / 29

Location: Each point lies on the lower abdomen 2 cun lateral to the midline.
- ST-26 lies 1 cun inferior to the umbilicus
- ST-27 lies 2 cun inferior to the umbilicus
- ST-28 lies 3 cun inferior to the umbilicus
- ST-29 lies 4 cun inferior to the umbilicus

Needling: Perpendicular or oblique insertion 1 to 1.5 cun

Note: (i) Deep penetration may penetrate the peritoneum (ii) Use all lower abdominal points with caution in pregnancy

Uses: *Regulates Qi* and treats the underlying organs ST-29 is used for gynaecological disorders, amenorrhea, and infertility.

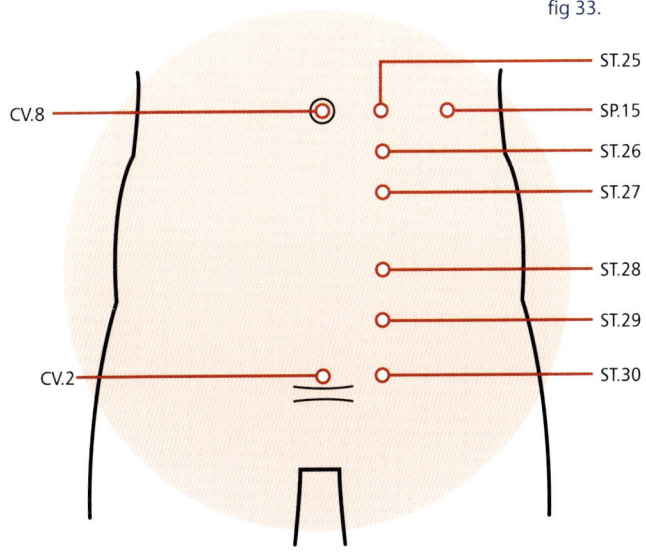

fig 33.

ACUPUNCTURE POINTS

STOMACH 30

Location: 2 cun lateral to the midline, level with the superior border of the symphysis pubis (fig 34).

Needling: Oblique or perpendicular insertion 1 to 1.5 cun.

Uses: (i) Meeting point of the Stomach channel with the Penetrating vessel (ii) used in the treatment of infertility (iii) traditionally used to *disperse Qi stagnation*.

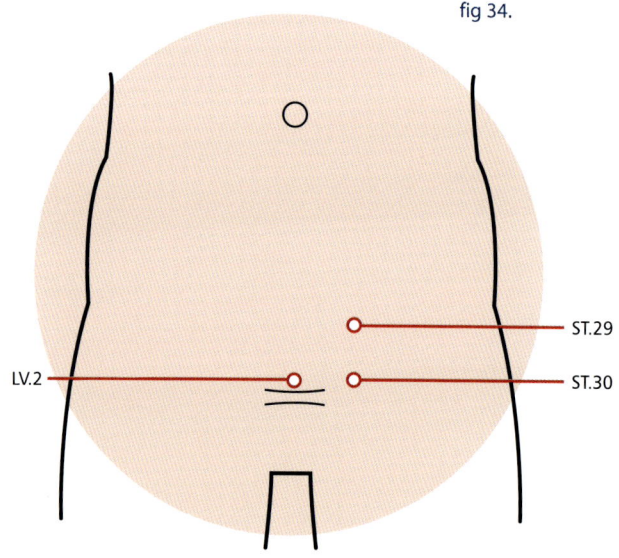

fig 34.

ACUPUNCTURE POINTS

STOMACH 31

Location: At the junction of a vertical line drawn down from the anterior superior iliac spine (ASIS), and a horizontal line drawn between the centre of the greater trochanter and the lower border of the pubic symphysis (fig 35).

Needling: Perpendicular insertion 1 to 2 cun

Note: (i) This point lies in a shallow depression just lateral to the Sartorius muscle.

Uses: (i) Anterior hip pain (ii) Traditionally known as the gateway to the thigh and used to *regulate qi and blood* when treating pain / numbness in the whole leg.

STOMACH 32

Location: On the anterior thigh, on a line connecting the lateral border of the patella and the ASIS. 6 cun (2 hand widths) proximal to the superior border of the patella (fig 35).

Needling: Perpendicular 1 to 2 cun

Uses: Pain in the quadriceps and anterior thigh.

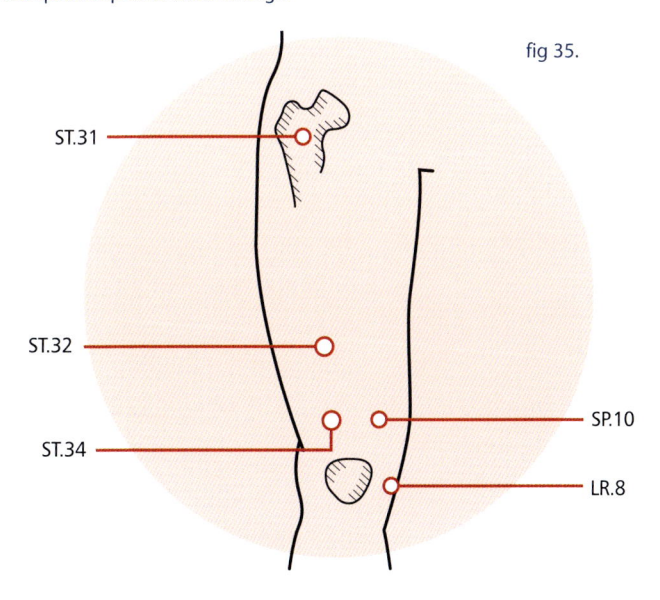

fig 35.

ACUPUNCTURE POINTS

STOMACH 33

Location: On the anterior thigh, on a line connecting the lateral border of the patella and the ASIS. 3 cun (1 hand width) proximal to the superior border of the patella (fig 36).

Needling: Perpendicular 1 to 2 cun

Uses: Pain in the quadriceps and anterior thigh.

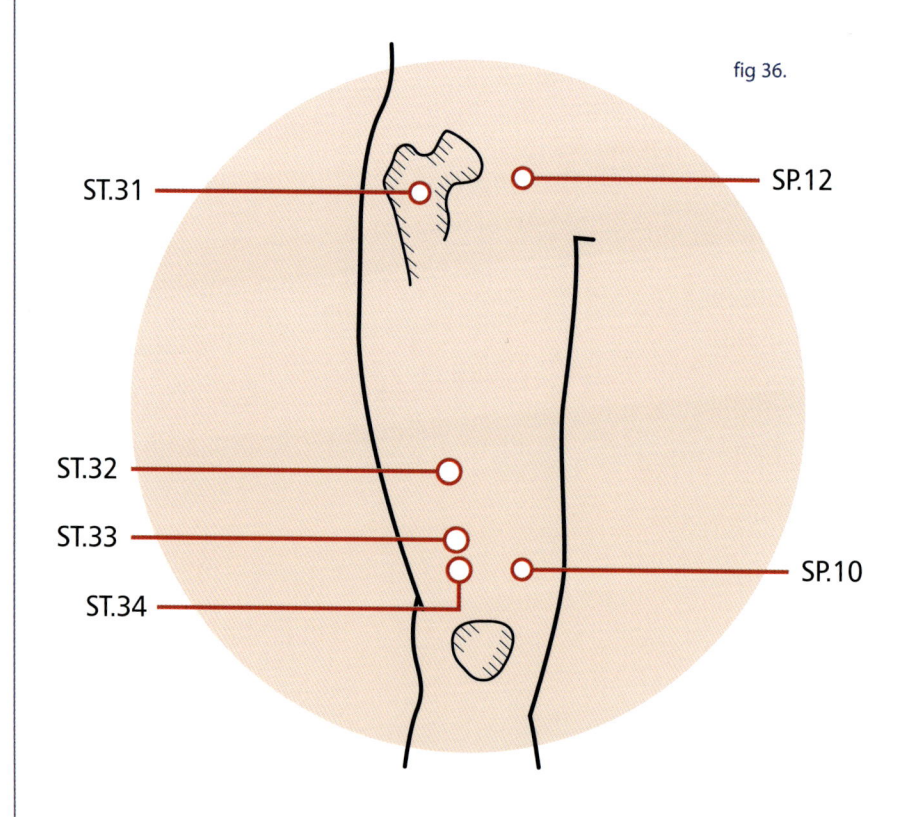

fig 36.

ACUPUNCTURE POINTS

STOMACH 34

Location: On the anterior thigh, on a line connecting the lateral border of the patella and the ASIS. 2 cun proximal to the superior border of the patella (fig 37).

Needling: Perpendicular 1 to 1.5 cun

Note: This point lies at the same horizontal level as SP-10

Uses: (i) Knee pain, acute stomach pain. (ii) *Xi-cleft* point of the Stomach channel

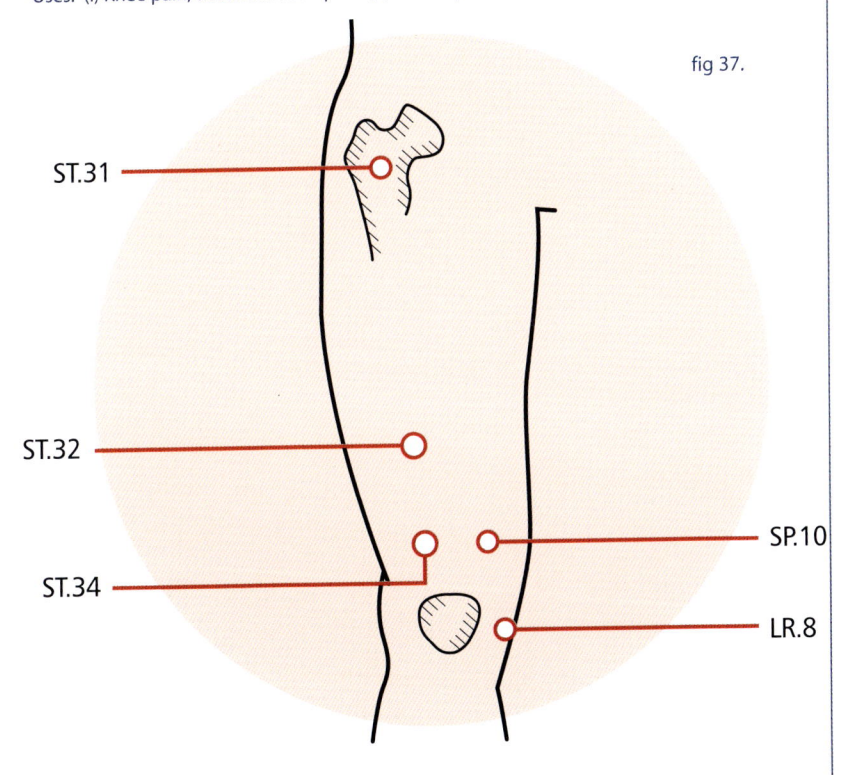

fig 37.

ST.31
ST.32
ST.34
SP.10
LR.8

ACUPUNCTURE POINTS

STOMACH 35

Location: When the knee is flexed, the point lies in the depression below the patella and lateral to the patellar ligament (fig 38).

Needling: Perpendicular insertion, directed towards the centre of the knee 1 to 2 cun, or medial oblique insertion 0.5-1.0 cun.

Note: The location of ST-35 corresponds to the arthroscopic access point to the knee. Deep insertion places the needle tip intra-articularly, so sterile practice is essential.

Uses: This point is the lateral 'eye' of the knee (*Xiyan* point). Used with the medial *Xiyan* point for knee pain and patellar tendon pain.

STOMACH 36

Location: Below the knee, 3 cun inferior to the lateral infrapatellar sulcus (ST-35) and 1 finger width lateral to the anterior crest of the tibia. The point lies level with the distal edge of the tibial tuberosity (fig 38).

Needling: Perpendicular insertion 1 to 1.5 cun

Note: This point is also a trigger point of Tibialis Anterior

Uses: (i) Strengthens the whole body and enhances the immune system. (ii) Used for dysfunctions of digestion. (iii) *Heavenly star* point for stomach and knee pain. (iv) Local point for anterior shin pain.

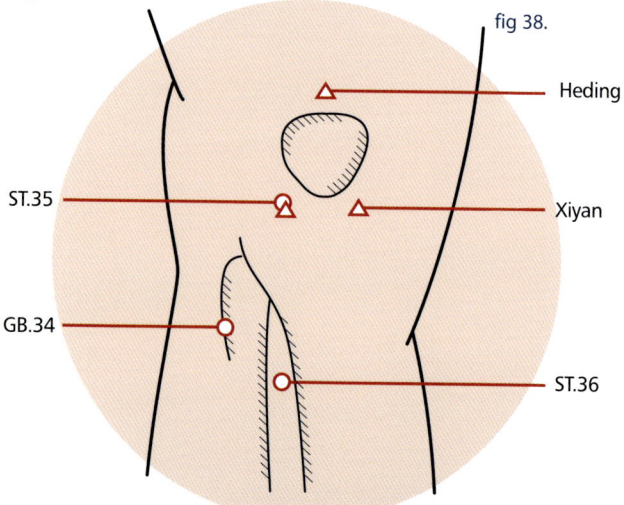

fig 38.

- Heding
- ST.35
- Xiyan
- GB.34
- ST.36

ACUPUNCTURE POINTS

STOMACH 37

Location: On the shin, 3 cun inferior to ST-36, and one finger-breadth lateral to the anterior crest of the tibia (fig 39).

Needling: Perpendicular 1 to 1.5 cun

Uses: (i) Used to treat anterior shin pain. (ii) *Lower Hi-Sea* point of the large intestine channel (iii) traditionally used to treat intestinal disorders.

STOMACH 38

Location: On the lower leg, midway between the knee joint line and the prominence of the lateral malleolus. The point lies one finger-breadth lateral to the anterior crest of the tibia (fig 39).

Needling: Perpendicular or oblique insertion 1 to 1.5 cun

Note: The midpoint of the tibia is most easily found clinically using the hand span method. The practitioner places the tips of their 5th (little) finger on the lateral malleolus and the lateral knee joint line. Spreading the hands equally, the thumbs come together over the tibial midpoint.

Uses: ST-38 is the classic frozen shoulder point. The point is needled, and the patient encouraged to actively rotate the shoulder within the limits of pain. As pain reduces, range of motion can increase.

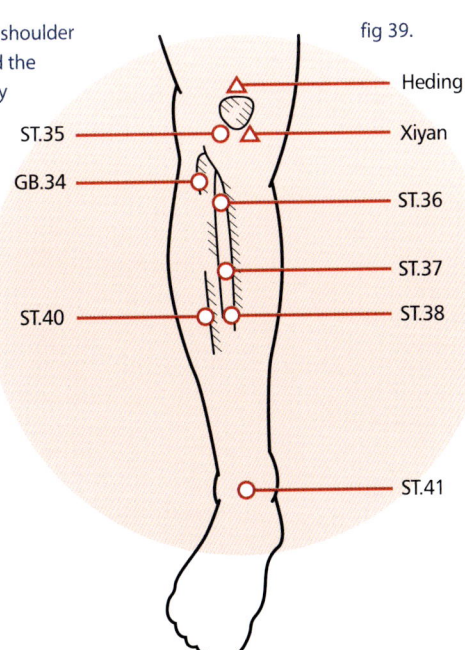

fig 39.

Labels: Heding, Xiyan, ST.35, GB.34, ST.36, ST.37, ST.40, ST.38, ST.41

STOMACH 39

Location: On the shin 1 cun inferior to ST-38, one finger-breadth lateral to the anterior crest of the tibia (fig 40).

Needling: Perpendicular insertion 1 to 1.5 cun

Uses: (i) *Lower He-Sea* point of the Small Intestine (ii) Traditionally used for lower abdominal pain, and back pain radiating to the testis.

STOMACH 40

Location: On the lower leg, midway between the knee joint line and the lateral malleolus, two finger breadths lateral to the anterior crest of the tibia, and one finger breadth lateral to ST-38 (fig 40).

Needling: Perpendicular or oblique insertion 1 to 1.5 cun

Uses: (i) *Luo-connecting point* of the Stomach channel (ii) Traditionally said to *transform phlegm and dampness* (iii) used to ease respiratory difficulty and production of sputum.

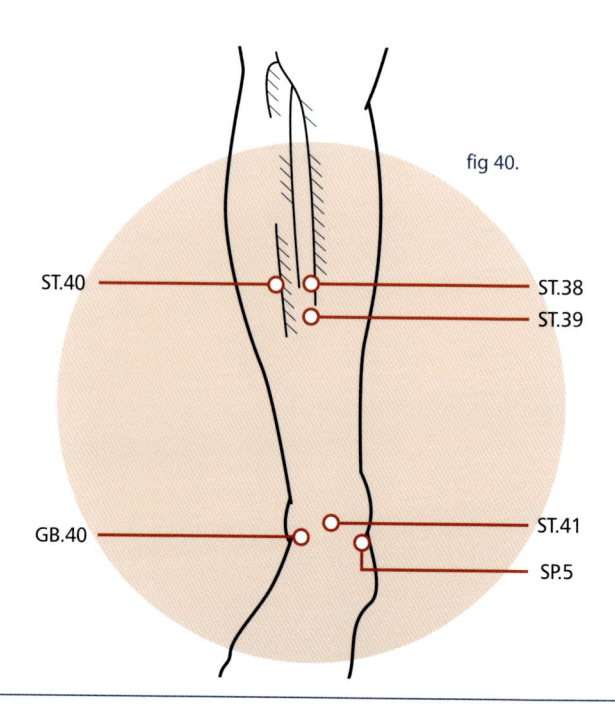

fig 40.

ACUPUNCTURE POINTS

STOMACH 41

Location: On the ankle, level with the apex of the lateral malleolus. The point lies in the depression between the tendons of extensor hallucis longus (EHL) and extensor digitorum longus (EDL) (fig 41)

Needling: Perpendicular insertion 0.5 cun.

Note: (i) To find this point ask the patient to pull their big toe (1st phalanx) up against resistance to activate EHL. The point lies lateral to this tendon. (ii) ST-41 lies directly over the anterior tibial vessels and nerve so deep needling must be avoided.

Uses: (i) *Jing-River* point of the Stomach channel (ii) Used mainly for conditions affecting the ankle joint.

STOMACH 42

Location: On the highest aspect of the dorsum of the foot in a small depression between the 2nd and 3rd metatarsals and the cuneiform bones. The point lies 1.5 cun distal to ST-41 (fig 41)

Needling: Oblique or perpendicular insertion 0.3-0.5 cun

Note: This point lies over the dorsalis pedis artery.

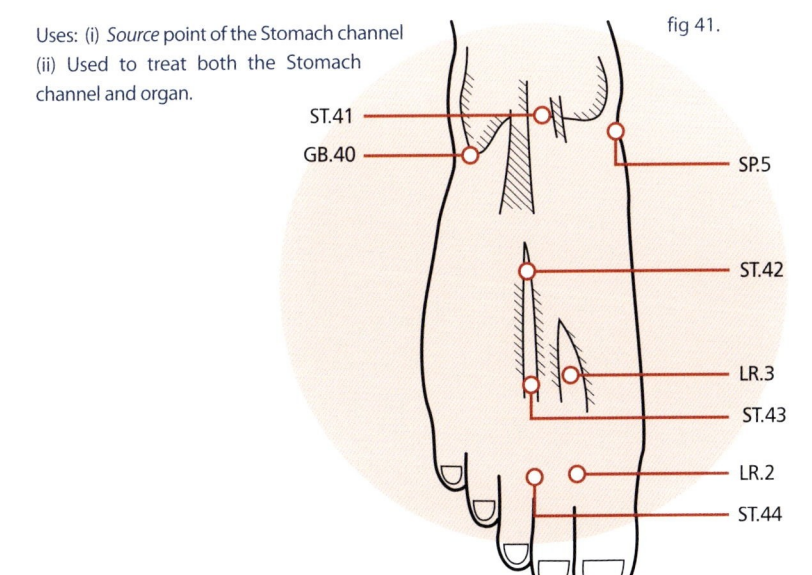

Uses: (i) *Source* point of the Stomach channel (ii) Used to treat both the Stomach channel and organ.

fig 41.

ST.41
GB.40
SP.5
ST.42
LR.3
ST.43
LR.2
ST.44

ACUPUNCTURE POINTS

STOMACH 43

Location: On the dorsum of the foot between the 2nd and 3rd toes. The point lies at the junction of the shaft and metatarsal head, approximately 1 cun proximal to ST-44 (fig 42).

Needling: Perpendicular or oblique insertion 0.5 to 1.0 cun

Uses: (i) local point for dorsal foot pain (ii) traditionally used to treat oedema (iii) said to *regulate* the Stomach, Spleen and Intestines.

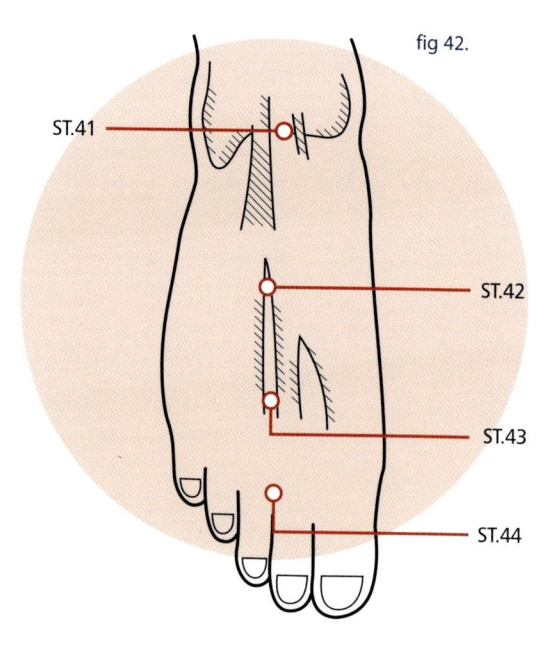

fig 42.

ACUPUNCTURE POINTS

STOMACH 44

Location: On the dorsum of the foot, between the second and third toes, 0.5 cun proximal to the interdigital skin web (fig 43).

Needling: Perpendicular insertion 0.3-0.5cun

Uses: (i) *Heavenly star* point for chills in the hands and feet. (ii) Traditionally used to clear the upper parts of the Stomach channel. (iii) Pain in the eye, lower teeth, and face. (iv) ST-44 is one of the *Bafeng* points used for swelling and pain in the toes.

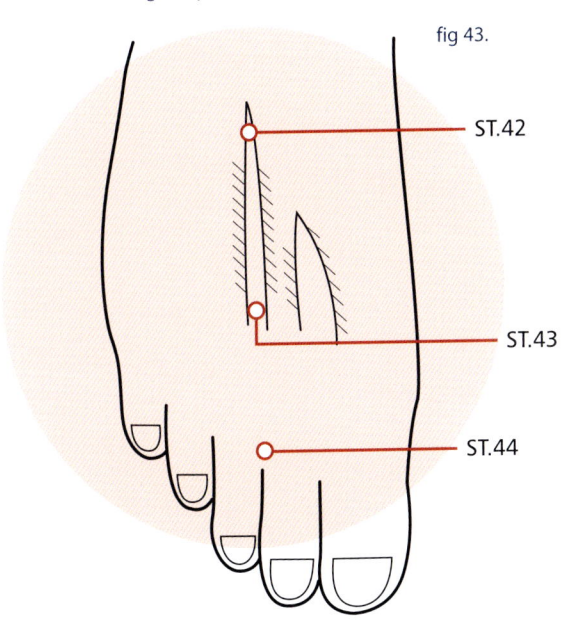

fig 43.

ST.42

ST.43

ST.44

STOMACH 45

Location: On the dorsal aspect of the 2nd toe at the junction of two lines drawn along the lateral border of the nail and the nail base (fig 44).

Needling: Perpendicular or oblique insertion 0.1-0.3 cun

Uses: (i) Nail or Tsing point of the Stomach channel (ii) traditionally used to *clear heat* in the Stomach channel and *calm the spirit*.

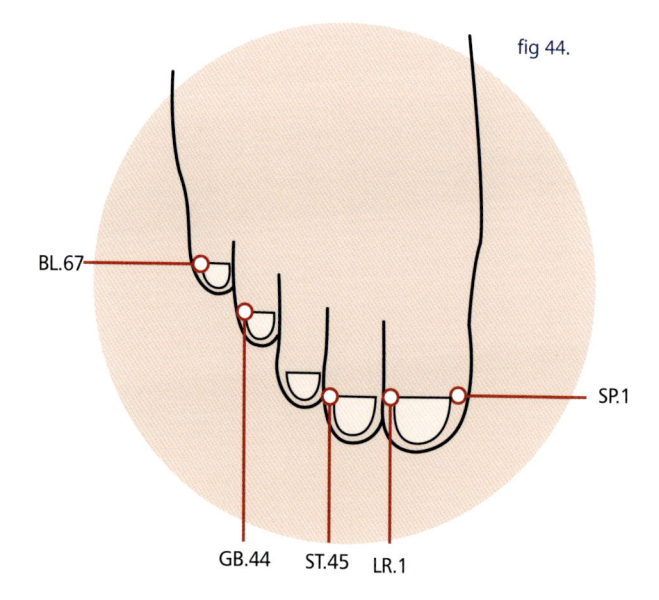

fig 44.

ACUPUNCTURE POINTS

SPLEEN (SP)

SPLEEN 1

Location: On the dorsal aspect of the 1st toe, at the intersection of lines drawn along the medial border of the nail and the nail base (fig 45).

Needling: Perpendicular insertion 0.1 to 0.2 cun.

Uses: (i) Nail point of the Spleen channel (ii) Traditionally used to stop bleeding including blood in the urine or stools.

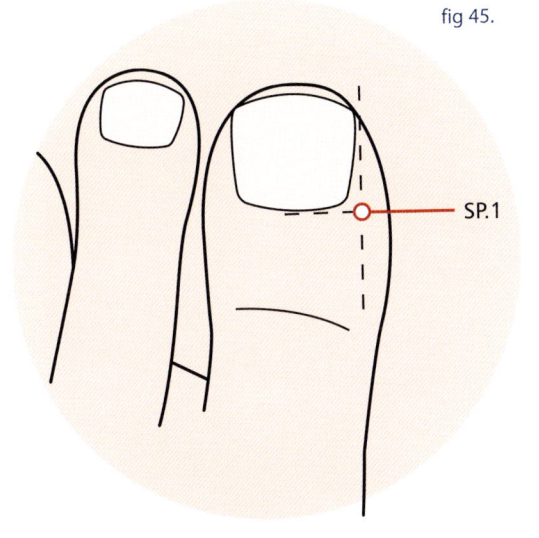

fig 45.

ACUPUNCTURE POINTS

SPLEEN 2

Location: On the medial aspect of the foot, distal to the head of the 1st metatarsal bone. The point lies at the junction of the shaft and base of the bone (fig 46).

Needling: Oblique insertion 0.3-0.5 cun

Uses: Local point for 1st MP joint pain

SPLEEN 3

Location: On the medial aspect of the foot, proximal to the head of the 1st metatarsal bone. The point lies at the junction of the red and white skin (fig 46).

Needling: Perpendicular insertion 0.5 cun.

Uses: (i) Local point for 1st MP joint pain. (ii) *Source point* of the Spleen channel. (iii) Traditionally used to treat *dampness* presenting as heaviness in the body, and to manage gastric disorders.

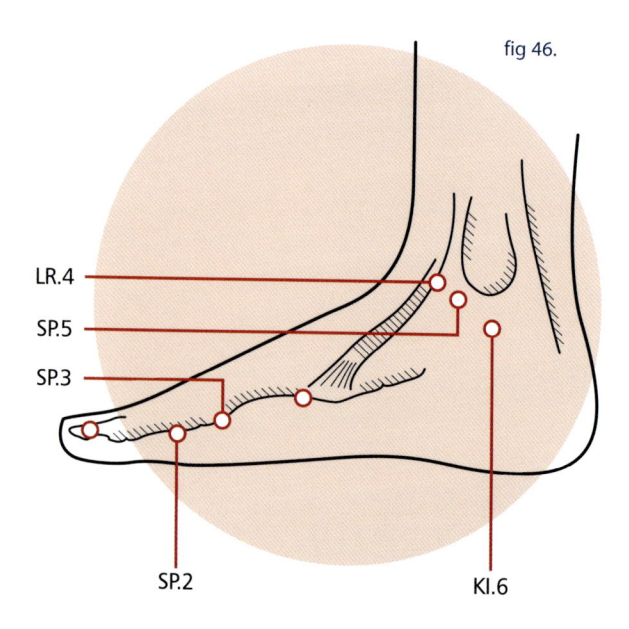

fig 46.

ACUPUNCTURE POINTS

SPLEEN 4

Location: On the medial aspect of the foot, in the depression distal to the base of the first metatarsal bone, close to the insertion of tibialis anterior. At the junction of the white and red skin (fig 47).

Needling: Perpendicular insertion 0.5 to 1 cun

Uses: (i) *Luo-connecting* point of the Spleen channel, *confluence point* of the Penetrating vessel. (ii) Traditionally used to treat abdominal distension and vomiting.

SPLEEN 5

Location: On the medial aspect of the ankle at the junction a vertical line drawn along the anterior border of the malleolus and a horizontal line drawn along the inferior border of the malleolus (fig 47).

Needling: Oblique or perpendicular 0.3-0.5 cun

Note: This point may also be located half way along a line drawn from the apex of the medial malleolus and the tubercle of Navicular.

Uses: (i) Medial eye of the ankle joint (ii) traditionally said to *fortify* the Spleen and *resolve dampness*.

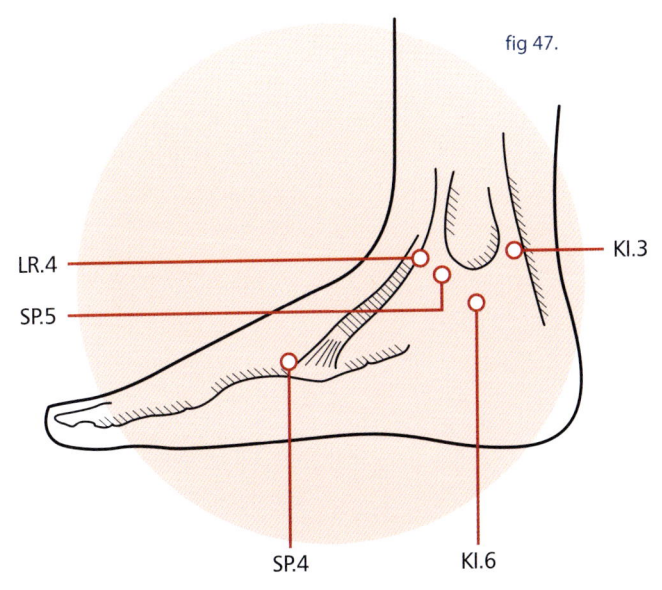

fig 47.

ACUPUNCTURE POINTS

SPLEEN 6

Location: On the medial side of the lower leg, 3 cun proximal to the apex of the medial malleolus. Just behind the medial crest of the tibia (fig 48).

Needling: Perpendicular insertion, 1 to 1.5 cun.

Note: (i) This point is said to be contraindicated in pregnancy especially when used with a *tonifying* technique. (ii) Often used to induce labour. (iii) May alter menstruation

Uses: (i) Meeting point of the 3 yin channels of the leg (Spleen, Liver, and Kidney). (ii) Said to *resolve dampness* including oedema and heaviness of the body. (iii) Used in many gynaecological disorders.

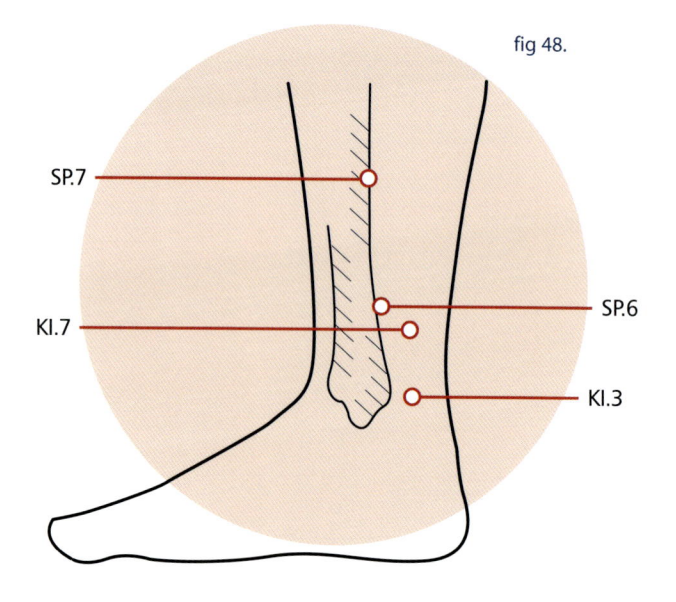

fig 48.

ACUPUNCTURE POINTS

SPLEEN 7
Location: On the medial side of the lower leg, 3 cun (one hand width) superior to SP-6, in the depression posterior to the medial tibial crest (fig 49).

Needling: Perpendicular or oblique insertion 1 – 1.5 cun

Uses: (i) local point for medial shin pain (ii) Traditionally said to fortify the spleen and *resolve dampness*.

SPLEEN 8
Location: Posterior to the medial crest of the tibia, 3 cun (one hand width) inferior to SP-9 (junction of the shaft and condyle of the tibia) (fig 49).

Needling: Perpendicular 1 to 1.5 cun

Uses: (i) *Xi-cleft* point of the Spleen channel (ii) Traditionally used for dysmenorrhoea.

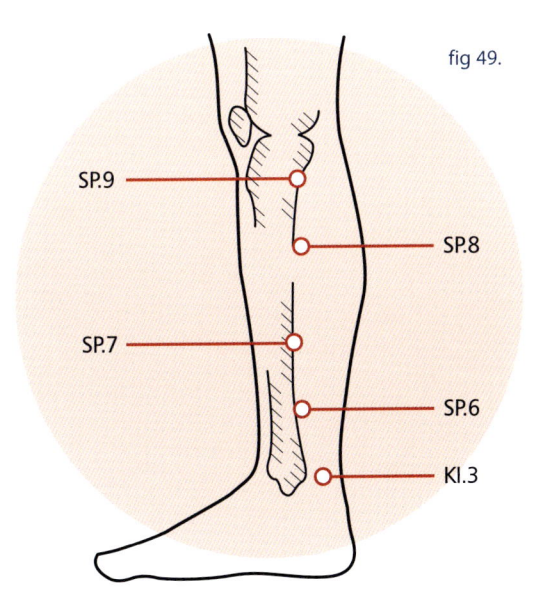

fig 49.

ACUPUNCTURE POINTS

SPLEEN 9

Location: Below the medial aspect of the knee, in the depression between the medial condyle of the tibia and its posterior border (fig 50).

Needling: Perpendicular insertion 1 to 1.5 cun

Note: SP-9 is located at the same level below the knee as GB-34

Uses: (i) *He-Sea and Water point* of the Spleen channel (ii) Main point to treat swelling in the legs.

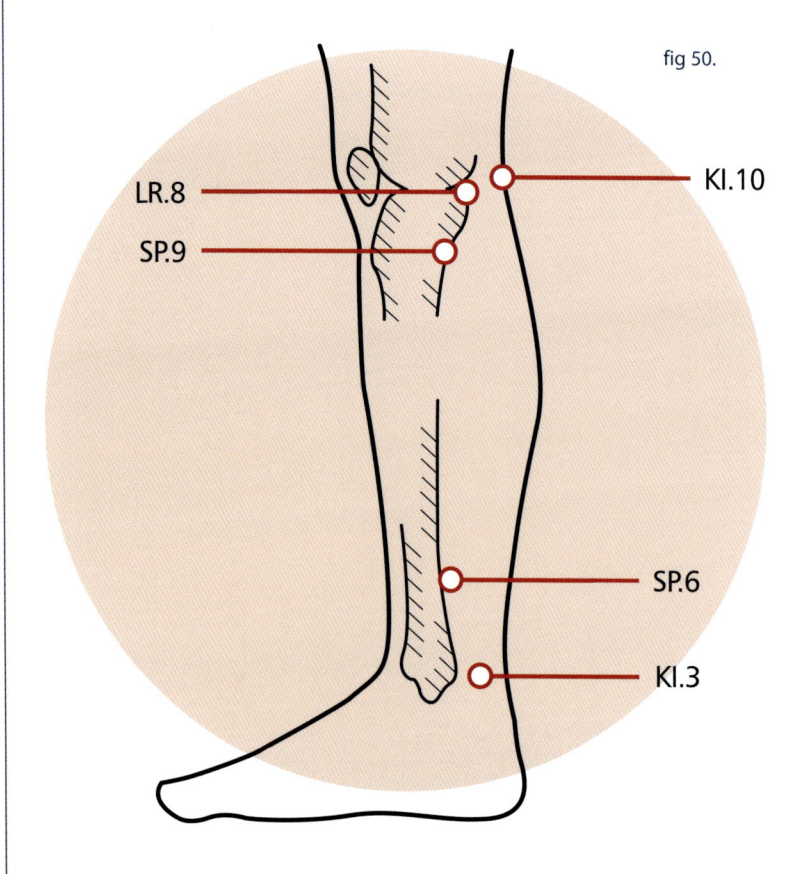

fig 50.

ACUPUNCTURE POINTS

SPLEEN 10
Location: 2 cun proximal to the superior border of the patella, in the centre of the vastus medialis obliquus (VMO) muscle (fig 51).

Needling: Perpendicular or oblique insertion 1 to 1.5 cun

Uses: (i) *Sea of blood* (ii) Traditionally used to invigorate the blood, eliminate blood stasis, and cool the blood (iii) Often used to treat skin conditions and itching.

SPLEEN 11
Location: On the medial side of the thigh 6 cun (two hand widths) above SP-10 (fig 51).

Needling: Perpendicular insertion 0.5-1.0 cun.

Note: Deep needling may puncture the femoral artery or vein

Uses: (i) Local point for pain in the Rectus femoris or Sartorius muscles (ii) Traditionally said to *drain dampness* and *clear heat* (iii) Used to treat disorders of urination.

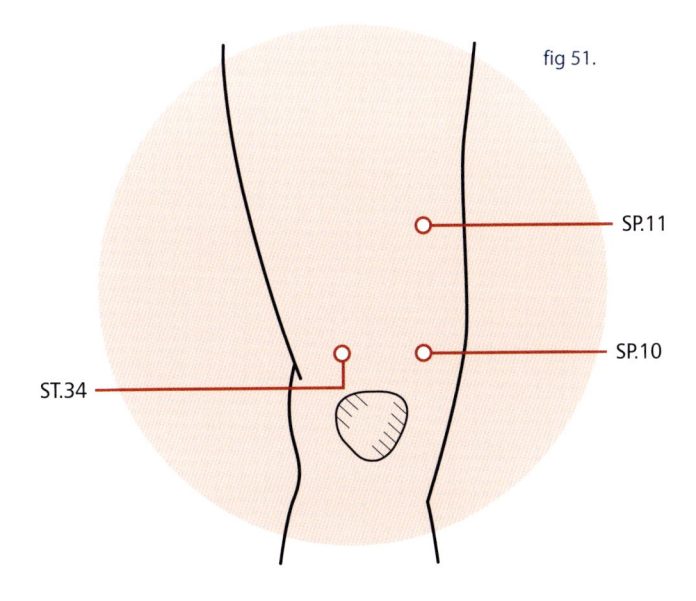

fig 51.

ACUPUNCTURE POINTS

SPLEEN 12

Location: Level with the upper border of the symphysis pubis, 3.5 cun lateral to the midline. The point is superior to the lateral edge of the inguinal ligament and lateral to the femoral artery (fig 52).

Needling: Perpendicular 0.5 – 1.0 cun along the channel.

Note: (i) Palpate for the femoral pulse and surface mark this before needling. (ii) needling in a medial direction endangers the femoral artery, and in a lateral direction the femoral nerve.

Uses: (i) May be used as a local point over the head of the femur. (ii) Traditionally used to treat inguinal hernia. (iii) Meeting point of the Yin Linking vessel with the Spleen and Liver channels.

SPLEEN 13

Location: 0.5 cun lateral and 0.7 cun superior to SP-12, in a shallow depression within the inguinal groove (fig 52).

Needling: Perpendicular insertion 0.5-1 cun

Note: Deep needling may penetrate the peritoneum

Uses: (i) Local point to alleviate pain (ii) Traditionally used to *disperse accumulation* and *regulate Qi* in the treatment of abdominal fullness and constipation.

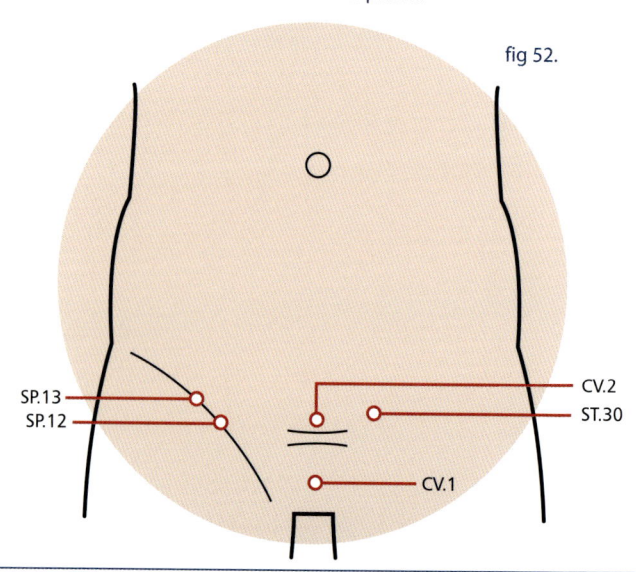

fig 52.

ACUPUNCTURE POINTS

SPLEEN 14 / 15 / 16

Location: Each point lies 4 cun from the midline (mamillary line) (fig 53).
SP-15 lies at the level of the umbilicus
SP-14 lies 1.3 cun inferior to the umbilicus
SP-16 lies 3 cun superior to the umbilicus

Needling: Perpendicular insertion 0.5-1 cun

Note: (i) Deep needling may penetrate the peritoneal cavity. (ii) SP-14 may be tender in cases of appendicitis (iii) the following points may be found at the level of the umbilicus at a distance from the midline (CV-8 midline). KI-16 (0.5 cun), ST-25 (2 cun) SP-14 (4 cun), GB-26 (free end of 11th rib).

Uses: (i) as local points for pain in the abdominal musculature (ii) traditionally used to alleviate *cold, damp* and *fullness* in the abdomen

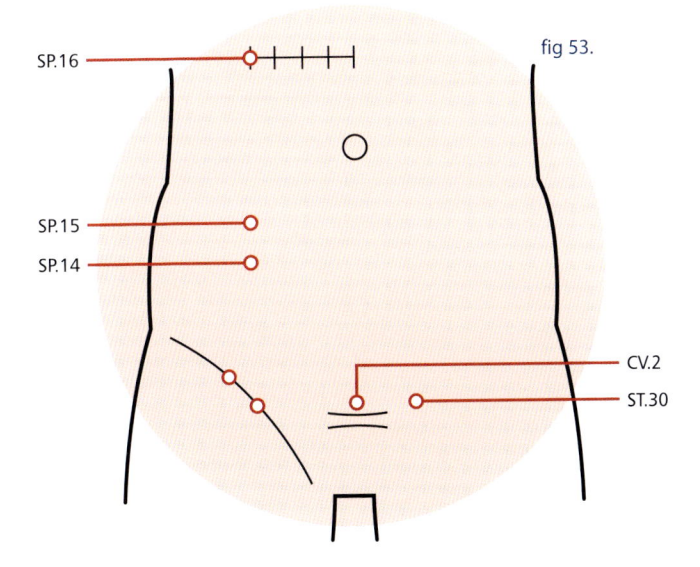

fig 53.

SP.16
SP.15
SP.14
CV.2
ST.30

ACUPUNCTURE POINTS

SPLEEN 17 / 18 / 19 / 20

Location: Each point is located 6 cun lateral to the midline (fig 54).
SP-17 lies in the 5th intercostal space
SP-18 lies in the 4th intercostal space
SP-19 lies in the 3rd intercostal space
SP-20 lies in the 2nd intercostal space

Needling: Transverse or oblique insertion along the intercostals space, 0.5 to 0.8 cun.

Note: (i) Deep insertion may cause pneumothorax (ii) In the male the nipple lies at the level of the 4th intercostal space, and as the intercostal space curves upwards SP-17 may be located 2 cun lateral to the nipple.

Uses: Used for general gastric pain including intercostal neuralgia.

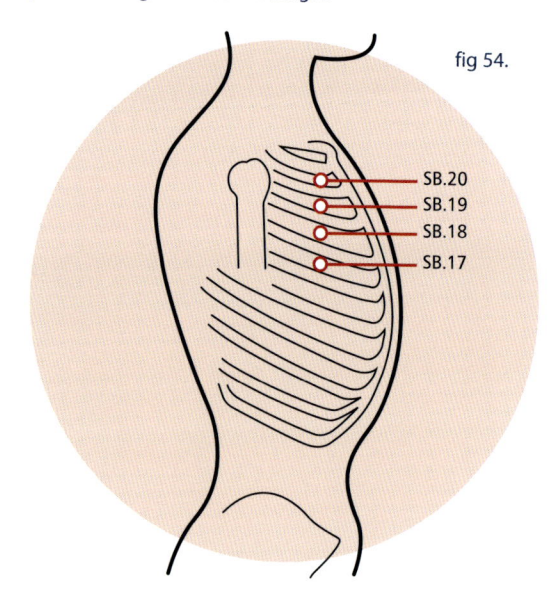

fig 54.

ACUPUNCTURE POINTS

SPLEEN 21

Location: On the mid axillary line in the 6th or 7th intercostal space. The point lies midway between the axilla and the 11th rib (fig 55).

Needling: Transverse or oblique insertion along the intercostals space, 0.5 to 0.8 cun.

Uses: (i) Great Luo-connecting point of the Spleen (ii) Traditionally said to assist the distribution of blood and Qi to the whole body.

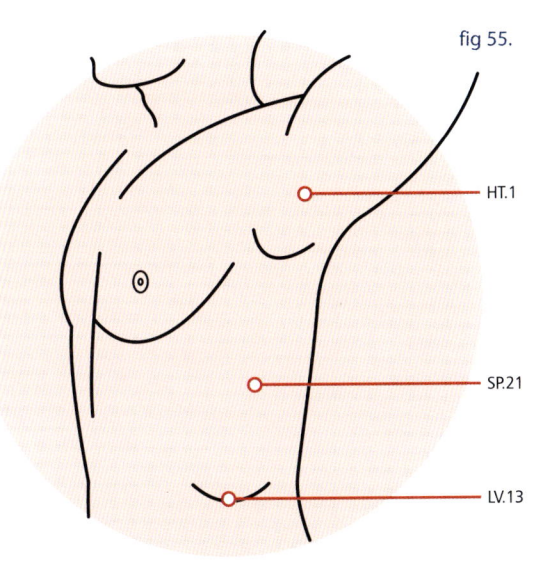

fig 55.

HT.1

SP.21

LV.13

ACUPUNCTURE POINTS

HEART (HT)

HEART 1

Location: In the centre of the axilla with the arm fully abducted (fig 56).

Needling: Perpendicular insertion 0.5-1.0 cun towards GB-21

Note: HT-1 lies at the highest point of the hollow, medial to the axillary artery

Uses: (i) Traditionally said to unbind the chest and open the channel

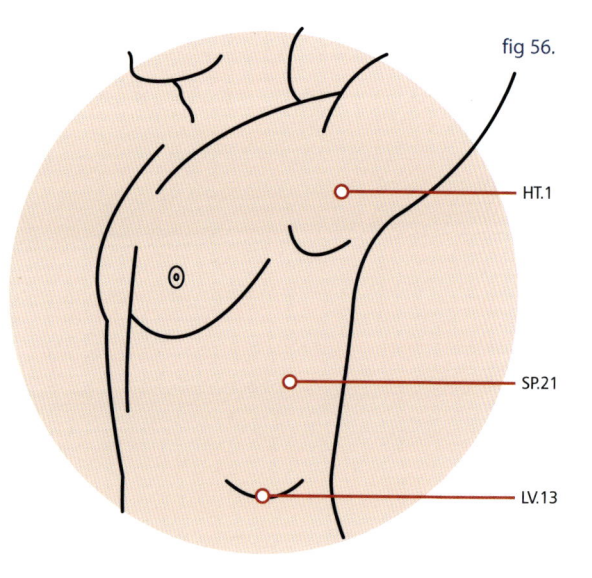

fig 56.

- HT.1
- SP.21
- LV.13

ACUPUNCTURE POINTS

HEART 2

Location: On a line joining HT-1 in the axilla to HT-3 at the elbow, HT-2 lies 3 cun (one hand width) proximal to HT-3 (fig 57).

Needling: Oblique or perpendicular insertion 0.5-1.0 cun

Note: The point lies in a groove medial to the biceps muscle, and is close to the brachial artery.

Uses: Used to alleviate local arm pain.

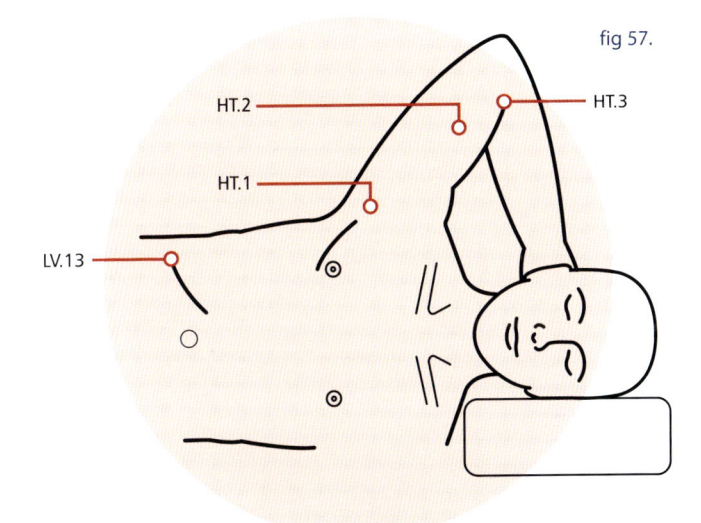

fig 57.

ACUPUNCTURE POINTS

HEART 3

Location: Midway between the biceps tendon and the medial epicondyle of the humerus. The point lies at the medial end of the elbow (transverse cubital) crease when the joint is fully flexed (fig 58).

Needling: 0.5 – 1.0 cun perpendicular insertion.

Uses: (i) Local point for golfers elbow. (ii) Used for pain / tremor in the hand. (iii) Traditionally said to *transform phlegm* and *calm the spirit*

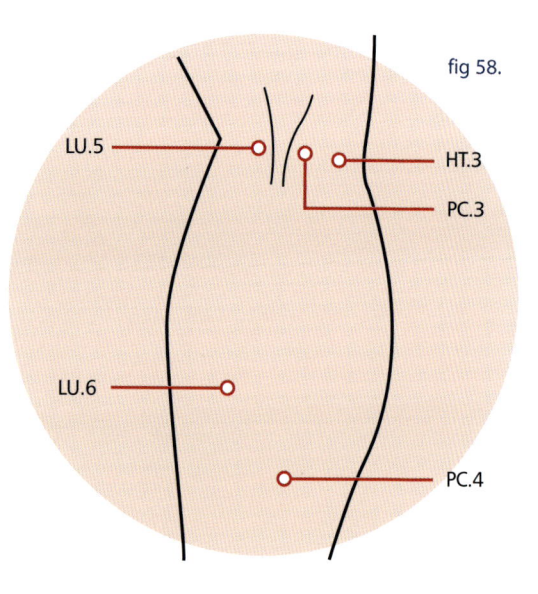

fig 58.

ACUPUNCTURE POINTS

HEART 4 / 5 / 6

Location: Each point lies on the radial side of the flexor carpi ulnaris (FCU) tendon, in relation to HT-7 at the wrist joint (fig 59).
Heart 4 lies 1.5 cun proximal to the wrist joint
Heart 5 lies 1 cun proximal to the wrist joint
Heart 6 lies 0.5 cun proximal to the wrist joint.

Needling: Perpendicular insertion 0.3 to 0.5 cun, or oblique insertion in a proximal or distal direction (along the meridian) 0.5-1 cun.

Uses: (i) Local ulnar sided wrist pain (ii) Traditionally used to *calm the spirit* in cases of anxiety (iii) HT-5 is the *Luo-connecting point* of the Heart channel and a *heavenly star point* (iv) HT-6 is the *Xi-cleft point*

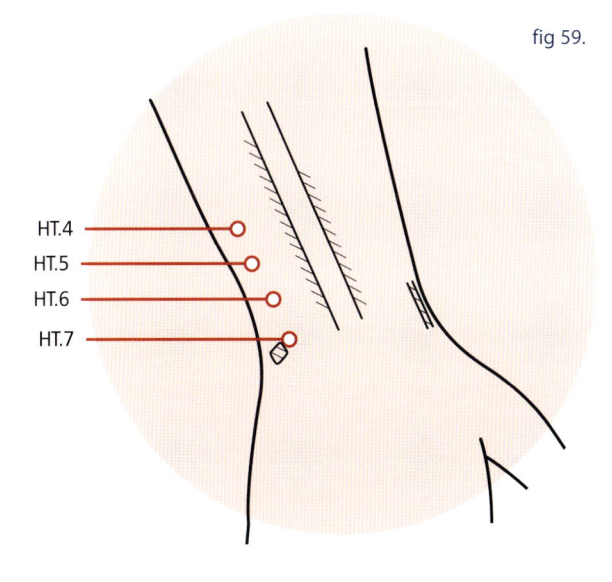

fig 59.

HT.4
HT.5
HT.6
HT.7

ACUPUNCTURE POINTS

HEART 7

Location: At the ulnar side of the wrist joint, in the depression between the pisiform bone (proximal border) and the radial side of flexor carpi ulnaris (FCU). (fig 60).

Needling: Perpendicular insertion 0.3 to 0.5 cun.

Note: The ulnar artery and nerve lie close to this point.

Uses: (i) Traditionally used to *calm the spirit*, especially in the treatment of insomnia. (ii) *Source point* for the heart channel.

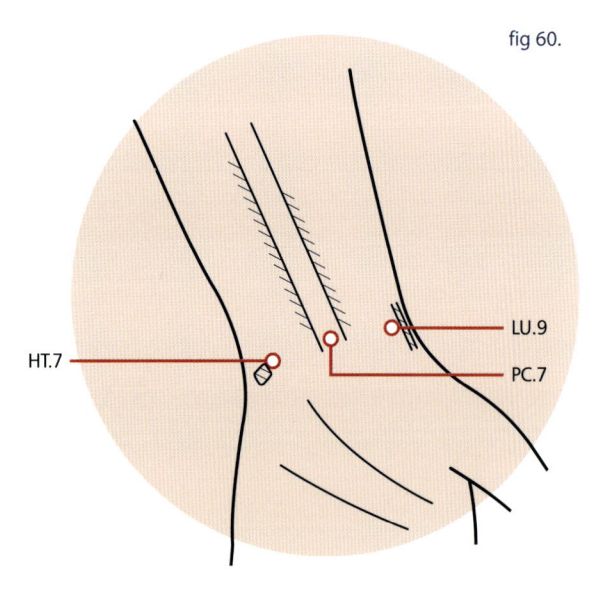

fig 60.

ACUPUNCTURE POINTS

HEART 8

Location: On the palm of the hand between the 4th and 5th metacarpal bones. Locate at the tip of the little finger when a fist is made (fig 61).

Needling: Perpendicular 0.5 cun

Note: HT-8 normally lies between the two transverse palmar creases on the ulnar aspect of the hand

Uses: (i) Local point for ulnar sided palm pain and finger contracture (ii) traditionally used to *clear heat* from the Heart and Small Intestine meridians.

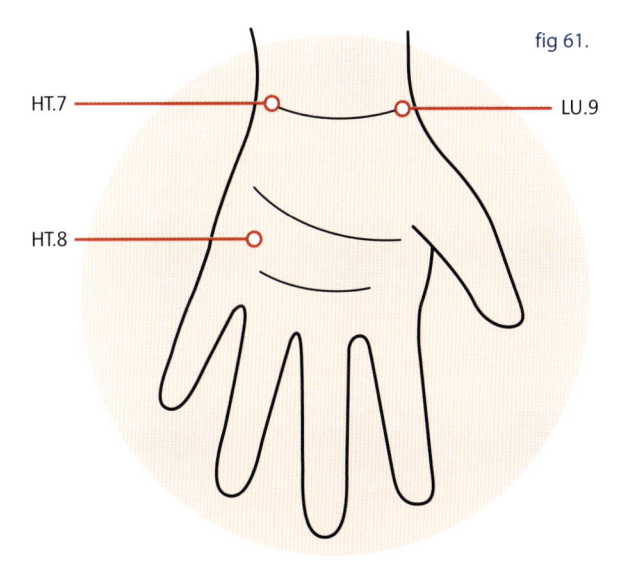

fig 61.

ACUPUNCTURE POINTS

HEART 9

Location: The radial nail point of the little finger (fig 62).

Needling: Perpendicular 0.1 to 0.2 cun.

Uses: Traditionally used to treat cardiac pain and palpitations.

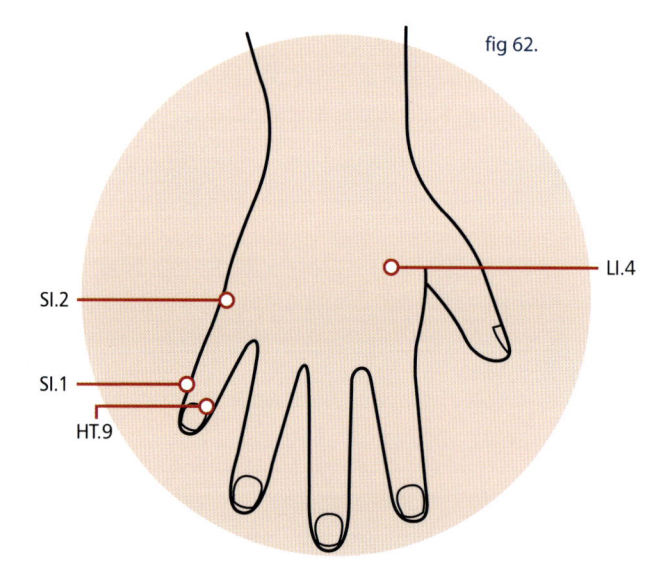

fig 62.

ACUPUNCTURE POINTS

SMALL INTESTINE (SI)

SMALL INTESTINE 1

Location: The ulnar nail point of the little finger. At the intersection of lines drawn along the ulnar border of the nail and the nail base (fig 63).

Needling: Perpendicular insertion 0.1 to 0.2 cun.

Uses: Traditionally used to treat headache and breast conditions including mastitis and insufficient lactation.

fig 63.

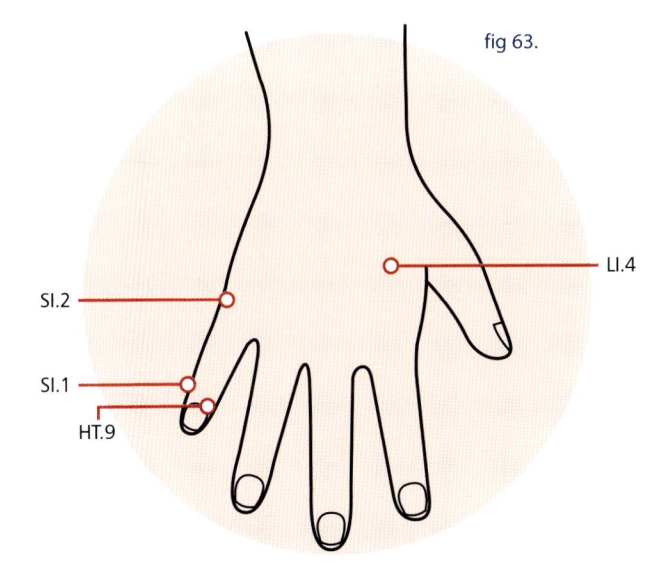

ACUPUNCTURE POINTS

SMALL INTESTINE 2 / 3

Location: On the ulnar border of the hand,
- SI-3 lies proximal to the head of the fifth metacarpal bone
- SI-2 lies distal to the head of the fifth metacarpal bone (fig 64).

Needling: Perpendicular insertion 0.3 - 0.5 cun. SI-3 may be needled more deeply (1.0 cun) towards the palm.

Note: Locate with the patient making a loosely clenched fist at the junction between the red and white skin

Uses: (i) Used to treat pain in the occiput and neck, occipital headache. (ii) SI-3 is the *confluence point* of the Governing vessel.

fig 64.

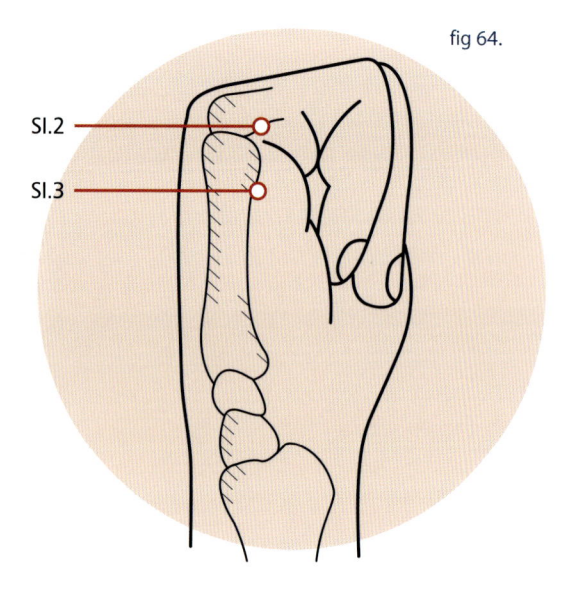

ACUPUNCTURE POINTS

SMALL INTESTINE 4 / 5

Location: on the Ulnar aspect of the hand in a depression between the base of the 5th metacarpal and the carpal bone (fig 65).
- SI-4 lies between the metacarpal and triquetral bone,
- SI-5 lies between the triquetral and the head of the ulna.

Needling: Perpendicular or oblique insertion 0.3-0.5 cun

Note. (i) SI-5 lies proximal to the pisiform bone at the level of the lateral wrist joint space. (ii) Palpation of both points is made easier by ulnar deviating the wrist.

Uses: (i) SI-4 is the *source* point of the Small Intestine channel. (ii) Both points are used as local points for lateral wrist joint pain.

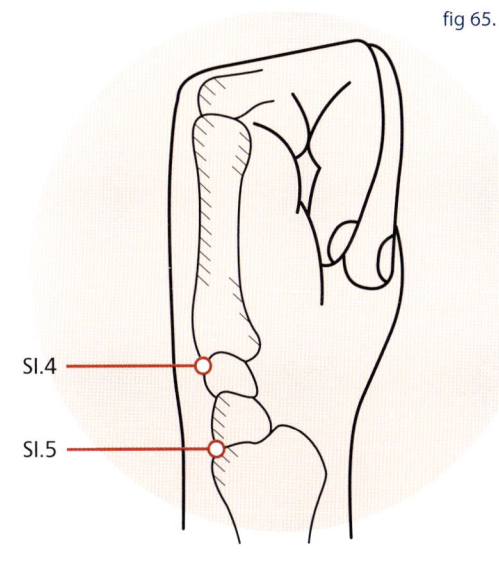

fig 65.

ACUPUNCTURE POINTS

SMALL INTESTINE 6

Location: On the ulnar side of the wrist proximal and radial to the ulnar styloid (fig 66).

Needling: Oblique or perpendicular 0.5 to 0.8 cun

Note: The traditional location method for this point is as follows. Ask the patient to put their palm flat on their chest. SI-6 is then located on the back of the wrist in a small cleft level with the styloid process of the ulna. This position half supinates the forearm and ulnar deviates the wrist to make the cleft deeper.

Uses: (i) *Xi-cleft* point of the Small Intestine channel (ii) Traditionally used to treat acute conditions of the posterior shoulder and arm. (iii) Said to *benefit the eyes* in the treatment of blurred vision in the elderly.

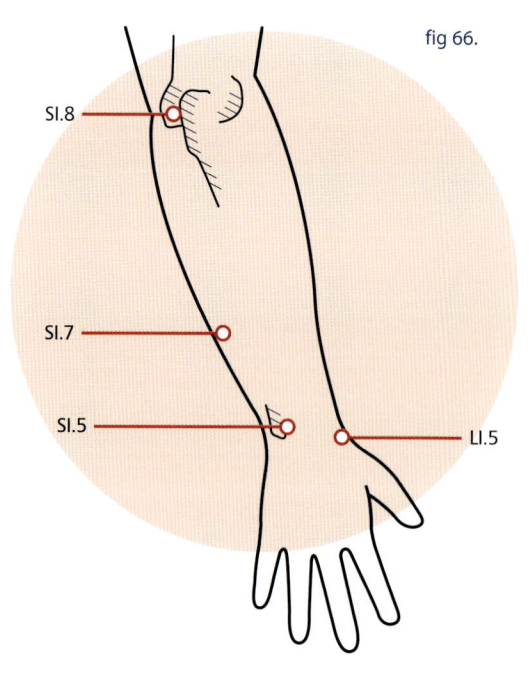

fig 66.

ACUPUNCTURE POINTS

SMALL INTESTINE 7
Location: On the line connecting SI-5 at the wrist to SI-8 at the elbow, small intestine 7 lies 5 cun proximal to the wrist joint. The point lies 1 cun distal to the midpoint of the line (fig 67).

Needling: Perpendicular insertion 0.5 – 1.0 cun

Note: SI-7 lies between the anterior border of the ulna and flexor carpi ulnaris (FCU)

Uses: (i) Local point for pain on the ulnar aspect of the forearm. (ii) *Luo-connecting* point of the Small Intestine.

SMALL INTESTINE 8
Location: In the depression between the olecranon process and the tip of the medial epicondyle of the humerus. The point lies immediately over the ulnar nerve (fig 67).

Needling: Perpendicular insertion 0.3 to 0.5 cun

Uses: Local point for pain in the posterior / medial shoulder.

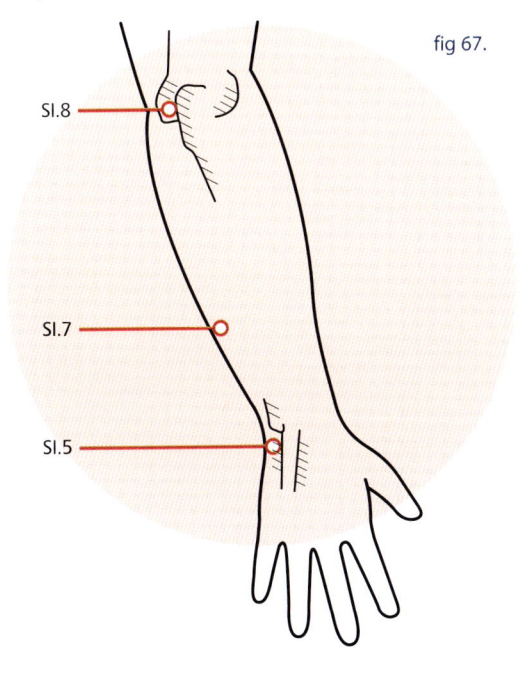

fig 67.

ACUPUNCTURE POINTS

SMALL INTESTINE 9

Location: On the posterior aspect of the shoulder, 1 cun superior to the posterior axillary crease (fig 68)

Needling: Perpendicular insertion 1 to 1.5 cun.

Note: (i) The point is located when the arm hangs relaxed by the side of the body. (ii) SI-9 is a trigger point for Teres Major

Uses: Local point for posterior shoulder pain.

SMALL INTESTINE 10

Location: On the posterior aspect of the shoulder, inferior to the scapular spine and directly over the head of the humerus. The point lies superior to the posterior axillary crease (SI-9) with the arm relaxed by the side of the body. (fig 68)

Needling: Perpendicular insertion 0.5 to 1.5 cun

Uses: (i) Its position directly over the head of the humerus makes SI-10 an important local point for posterior shoulder pain. (ii) *meeting point* of the Small Intestine, Large Intestine, Yang Linking and Yang Motility channels.

fig 68.

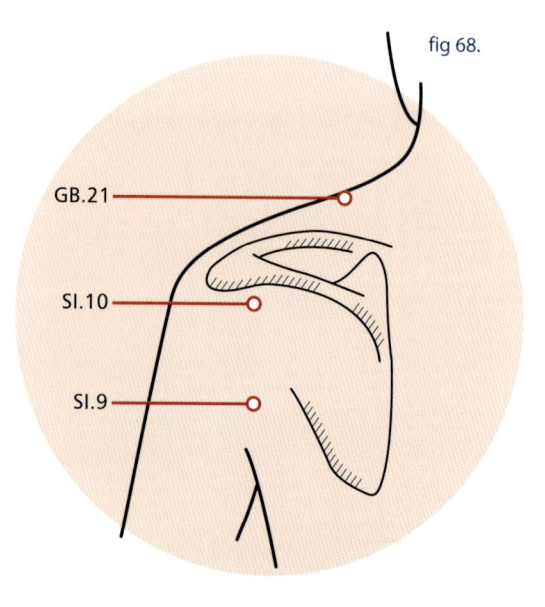

ACUPUNCTURE POINTS

SMALL INTESTINE 11

Location: In the centre of the infraspinous fossa. At the junction of the upper 1/3rd and lower 2/3rds of a line joining the midpoint of the scapular spine (inferior border) and the inferior angle of the scapula (fig 69).

Needling: Perpendicular or oblique insertion 0.5 to 1.5 cun

Note: SI-11 is a trigger point of the infraspinatus muscle.

Uses: Local point for scapular pain.

SMALL INTESTINE 12

Location: In the centre of the suprascapular fossa, directly above SI-11 (fig 69).

Needling: Perpendicular or oblique insertion 0.5 to 1 cun

Note: SI-12 is a trigger point of the supraspinatus muscle.

Uses: (i) Local point for scapular pain. (ii) *Meeting point* of the Small Intestine, Large Intestine, Triple Energiser, and Gall Bladder channels.

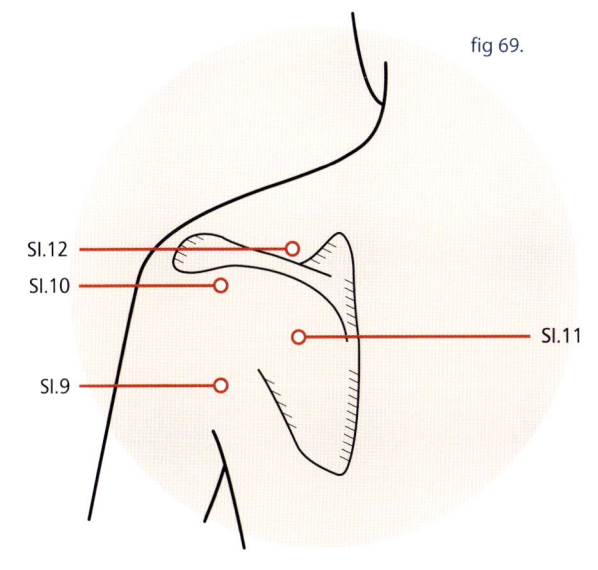

fig 69.

ACUPUNCTURE POINTS

SMALL INTESTINE 13

Location: In a small sulcus between the superior angle of the scapula and the superior-medial end of the scapular spine, close to the medial insertion of supraspinatus (fig 70)

Needling: Perpendicular or oblique insertion 0.3 – 1.0 cun

Note: SI-13 lies at the midpoint of a line joining the posterior shoulder joint (SI-10) and the spinous process of T2

Uses: Local point for posterior shoulder pain.

SMALL INTESTINE 14

Location: 3 cun lateral to the lower border of T1, approximately at the tip of the superior angle of the scapula. (fig 70)

Needling: Oblique insertion 0.3 to 0.5 cun directed towards the superior angle of the scapula.

Note: (i) Deep needling away from the Scapula carries the risk of pneumothorax (ii) SI-14 is a trigger point of the Levator scapulae muscle.

Uses: Pain at the superior angle of the scapula.

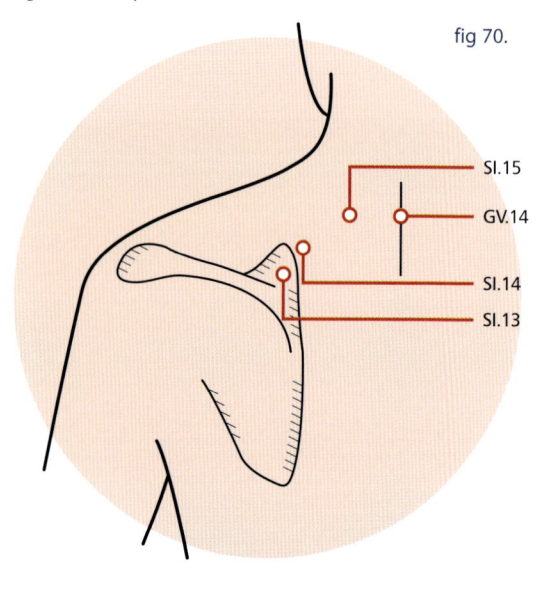

fig 70.

ACUPUNCTURE POINTS

SMALL INTESTINE 16
Location: Level with the Adam's apple (Laryngeal prominence) on the posterior border of Sternocleidomastoid (SCM) muscle (fig 71)

Needling: Perpendicular insertion 0.5 cun

Note: Three points lie on a line level with the laryngeal prominence LI-18, SI-16, and ST-9.

Uses: (i) traditionally used to treat the ears, throat, and voice.

SMALL INTESTINE 17
Location: Between the angle of the mandible and the anterior border of the sternocleidomastoid (SCM) muscle. The point lies anterior to the transverse process of C2 (fig 71).

Needling: Perpendicular or oblique insertion 0.5 to 0.8 cun.

Note: The carotid artery and jugular vein lie close to this point, so deep insertion should be avoided.

Uses: Neck and throat pain.

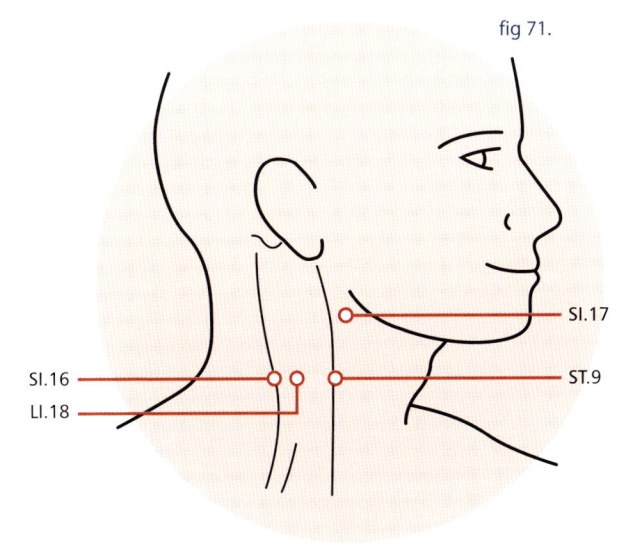

fig 71.

ACUPUNCTURE POINTS

SMALL INTESTINE 18

Location: Directly below the outer canthus of the eye, at the lower border of the zygomatic bone (fig 72).

Needling: 0.3 – 0.4 cun perpendicular or oblique.

Uses: (i) Often used for pain in the upper teeth and trigeminal neuralgia. (ii) *Meeting point* of the Small Intestine and Triple Energiser channels.

fig 72.

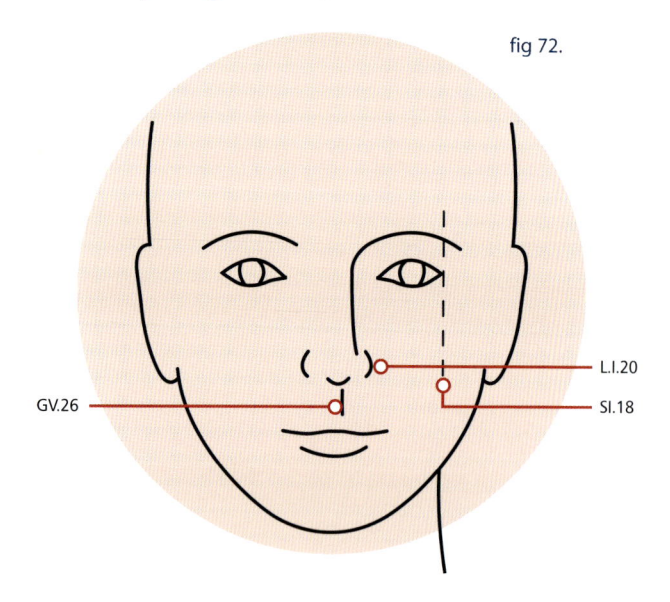

GV.26

L.I.20

SI.18

ACUPUNCTURE POINTS

SMALL INTESTINE 19

Location: With the mouth open, the point lies in the depression between the tragus and the condyloid process of the mandible (fig 73).

Needling: Perpendicular insertion 0.5 to 1 cun

Uses: (i) Ear and Temporomandibular joint (TMJ) pain. (ii) *Meeting point* of the Gall Bladder, Triple Energiser, and Small Intestine channels.

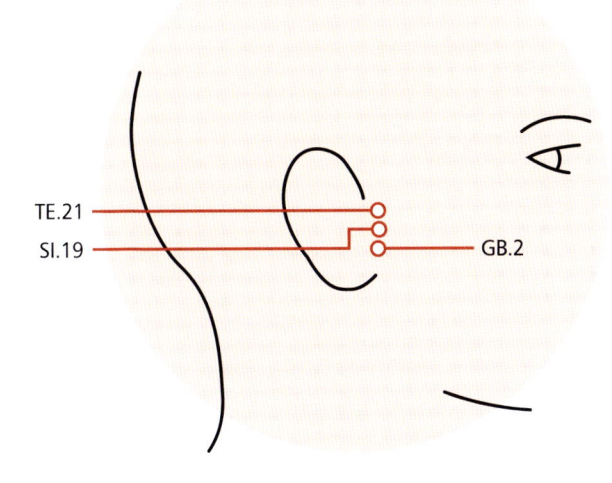

fig 73.

ACUPUNCTURE POINTS

BLADDER (BL)

BLADDER 1

Location: 0.1 cun superior and medial to the inner canthus of the eye (fig 74).

Needling: Perpendicular insertion 0.2 to 0.3 cun with the eyeball pushed downwards and sideways away from the needle.

Note: BL-2 is a safer alternative to this point.

Uses: Traditionally used to treat redness and swelling in the eye. Said to improve eyesight.

BLADDER 2

Location: In the depression at the medial end of the eyebrow, within a groove (incisura frontalis) of the supraorbital portion of the frontal bone (fig 74).

Needling: transverse / subcutaneous insertion 0.5 cun

Uses: BL-2 is used as a safer alternative to BL-1 for disorders of the eye and frontal headache.

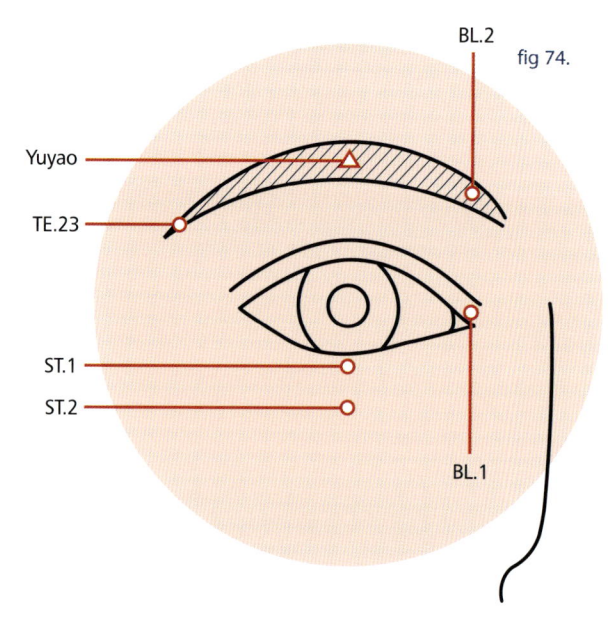

fig 74.

ACUPUNCTURE POINTS

BLADDER 3

Location: Vertically above the medial canthus of the eye (BL-2) 0.5 cun within the anterior hairline (fig 75)

Needling: Transverse insertion 0.5- 1.0 cun along the channel

Uses: Local point used in the treatment of Frontal headache.

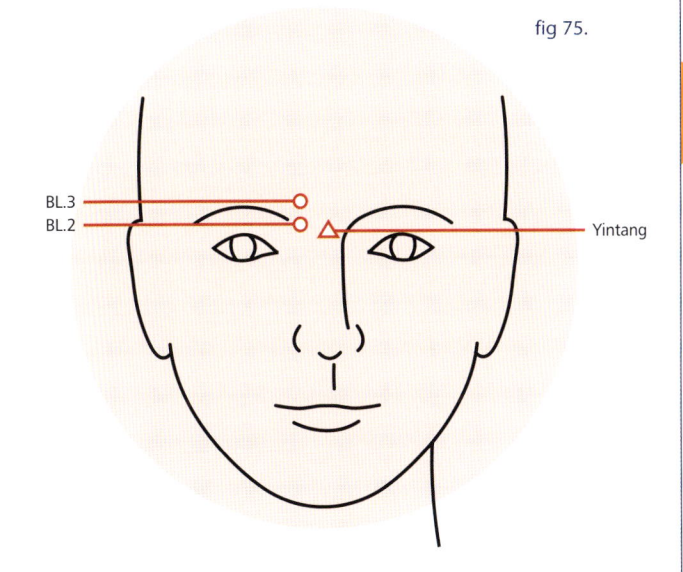

fig 75.

ACUPUNCTURE POINTS

BLADDER 4 / 5 / 6 / 7 / 8

Location: 1.5 cun lateral to the midline, each point is at a distance from the anterior hairline (fig 76)
- BL-4 lies 0.5 cun from the anterior hairline
- BL-5 lies 1.0 cun from the anterior hairline
- BL-6 lies 2.5 cun from the anterior hairline
- BL-7 lies 4 cun from the anterior hairline
- BL-8 lies 5.5 cun from the anterior hairline

Needling: Transverse insertion 0.5- 1.0 cun along the channel.

Note: In the case of baldness where the anterior hairline is no longer present, ask the patient to raise their eyebrows. The original hairline is found where the furrows formed in the loose forehead skin meet the tighter scalp.

Uses: (i) Local points for headache (ii) Traditionally used to the *eliminate wind* and *heat* and so clear the head.

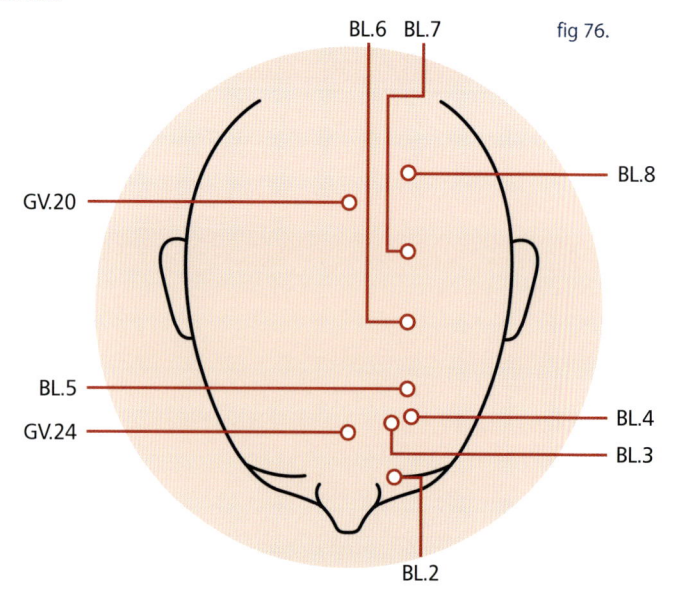

fig 76.

ACUPUNCTURE POINTS

BLADDER 9

Location: Level with the upper ridge of the external occipital protuberance, 1.3 cun lateral to the midline and 1.5 cun superior to GV-16 (craniocervical junction) (fig 77).

Needling: 0.3 cun subcutaneous

Uses: (i) BL-9 is a trigger point of the Semispinalis capitis muscle. (ii) Traditionally used to *eliminate wind* in the case of occipital headache.

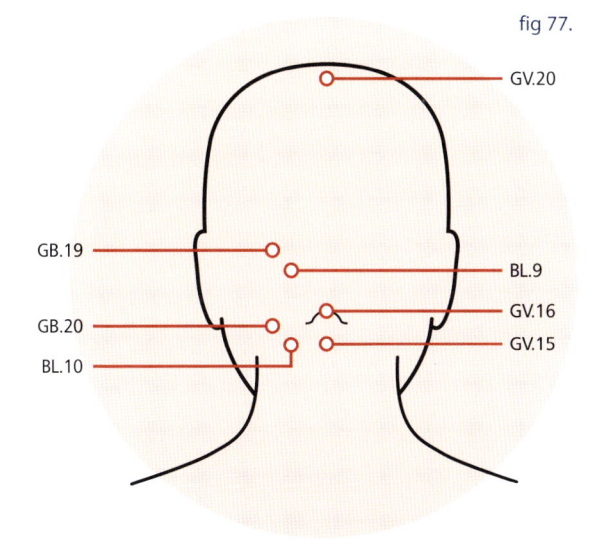

fig 77.

ACUPUNCTURE POINTS

BLADDER 10

Location: On the lateral aspect of the trapezius muscle, 1.3 cun lateral to the 1st cervical vertebral (C1) (fig 78).

Needling: Perpendicular insertion 0.5 cun.

Uses: (i) BL-10 may be used to release tension in the sub-occipital muscles common with a head forward posture. (ii) Often used clinically to treat dizziness (iii) *Window of Heaven* point traditionally used to treat *rebellious Qi rising to the head*.

fig 78.

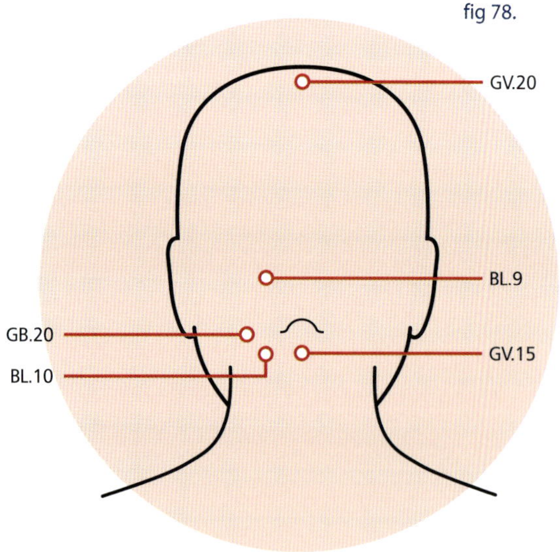

ACUPUNCTURE POINTS

BLADDER 11

Location: 1.5 lateral to the lower border of the spinous process of the first thoracic vertebra (T1), approximately level with the superior angle of the scapula (fig 79).

Needling: Oblique insertion medially towards the spine, 0.5 cun.

Note: (i) The three points BL-11 (bilateral) and GV-14 are sometimes called the 'dorsal magic triangle'. (ii) Bladder points may be remembered relative to the vertebrae.
- For points BL-11 to BL-17 the points are at the same level (BL-11 at T1, BL-12 at T2 etc).
- From BL-18 to BL-21 *add one* to the point (BL-18 at T9, BL-19 at T10 etc).
- From BL-22 the points are numbered in the lumbar spine by *subtracting one* (Bl-22 at L1, BL-23 at L2 etc).

Uses: (i) *Influential point* for bone. (ii) Often needled with GV-14 for a relaxing and calming effect.

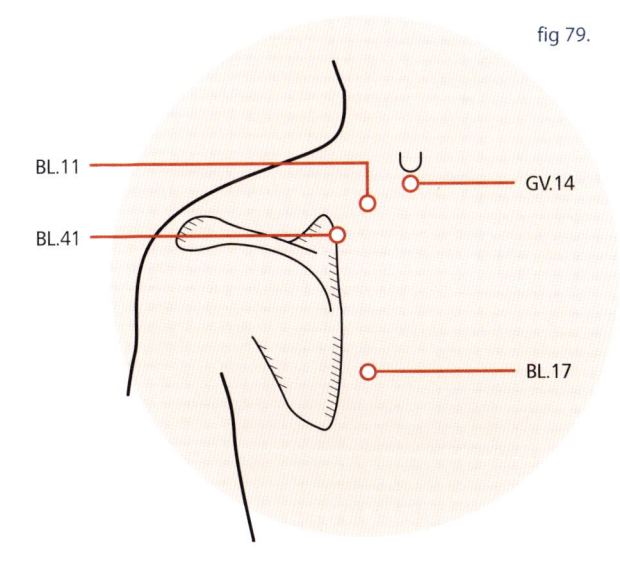

fig 79.

ACUPUNCTURE POINTS

BLADDER 12

Location: 1.5 cun lateral to the lower border of the spinous process of T2 (fig 80)

Needling: Oblique insertion medially towards the spine 0.5 cun

Uses: (i) Local points for spinal pain (ii) Meeting point of the Bladder and Governing vessels. (iii) traditionally used to *expel wind*.

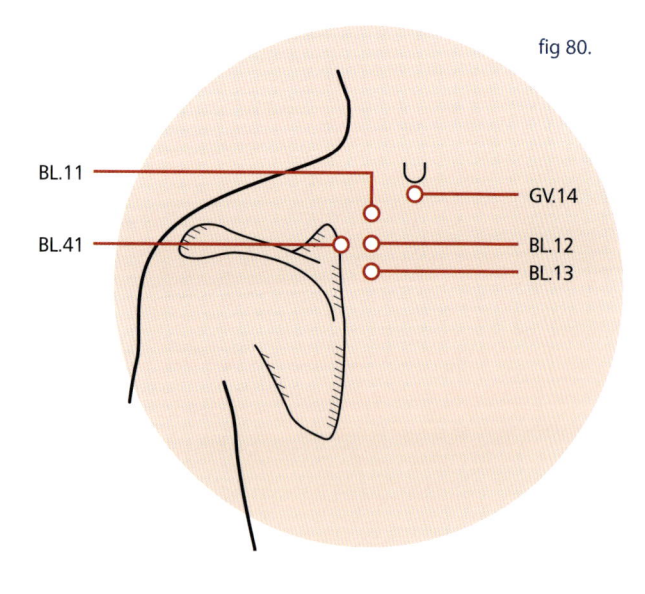

fig 80.

ACUPUNCTURE POINTS

BLADDER 13 – 22

Location: 1.5 cun lateral to the lower border of the spinous process of the corresponding vertebra (fig 81).

Needling: Oblique insertion medial towards the spine 0.5 cun.

Uses: (i) Local point for spinal pain (ii) Back Shu point related to the internal organs. Points are palpated and needled if painful.

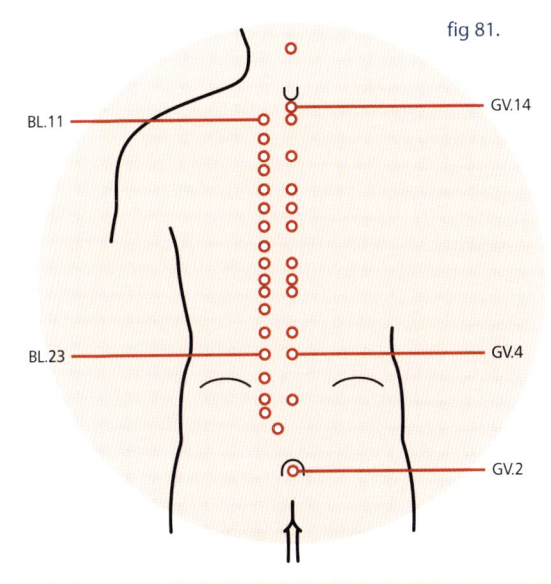

fig 81.

Point	Level	Shu	Point	Level	Shu
BL-13	T3	Lung	BL-20	T11	Spleen
BL-14	T4	Pericardium	BL-21	T12	Stomach
BL-15	T5	Heart	BL-22	L1	*Triple Energiser*
BL-16	T6	*Governing vessel*	BL-23	L2	Kidney
BL-17	T7	Diaphragm	BL-24	L3	*Sea of Qi*
BL-18	T9	Liver	BL-25	L4	Large Intestine
BL-19	T10	Gall Bladder	BL-26	L5	*Gate of Origin*

ACUPUNCTURE POINTS

BLADDER 27 / 28 / 29 / 30

Location: Each point lies 1.5 cun lateral to the midline, level with the corresponding posterior sacral foramen (fig 82).
- BL-27 level with the S1 foramen
- BL-28 level with the S2 foramen
- Bl-29 level with the S3 foramen
- BL-30 level with the S4 foramen

Needling: Perpendicular insertion 0.5 – 1.0 cun

Note: The S1 level lies just medial and slightly superior to the posterior superior iliac spine (PSIS) (fig 82).

Uses: (i) Local points for Lumbo-sacral pain (ii) Shu points for the Small Intestine (BL-27), Bladder (BL-28), and Mid spine (BL-29). (iii) Traditionally sacral points are used to *regulate Qi* of the Uterus and Genito-Urinary (GU) system.

fig 82.

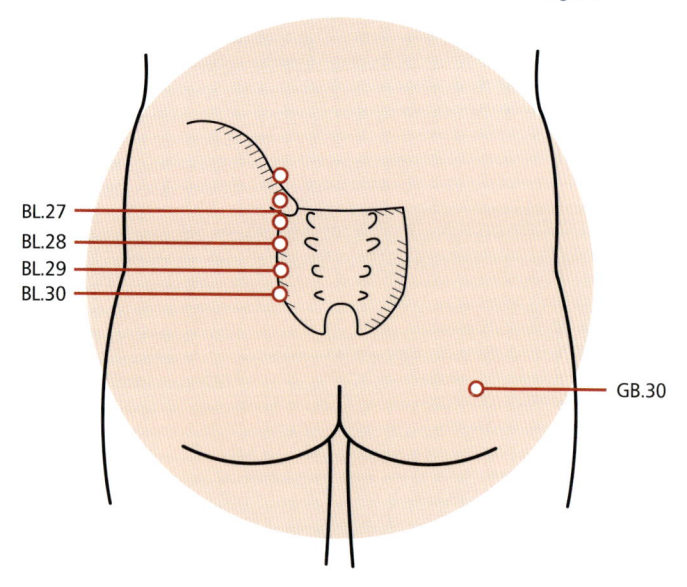

ACUPUNCTURE POINTS

BLADDER 31 / 32 / 33 / 34

Location: Within the corresponding posterior sacral foramen (fig 83).
- BL-31 within the S1 foramen
- BL-32 within the S2 foramen
- BL-33 within the S3 foramen
- BL-34 within the S4 foramen

Needling: Perpendicular insertion 0.8 – 1.2 cun

Note: BL-31 point lies at the midpoint between the posterior superior iliac spine (PSIS) and the midline.

Uses: (i) Local points for lumbo-sacral pain. (ii) Traditionally called the *4 crevice points* indicating their positions within the Sacral foramina (iii) often used in the treatment of urinary dysfunction, and menstrual disorders. (iv) *meeting points* of the Bladder and Gall bladder channels.

fig 83.

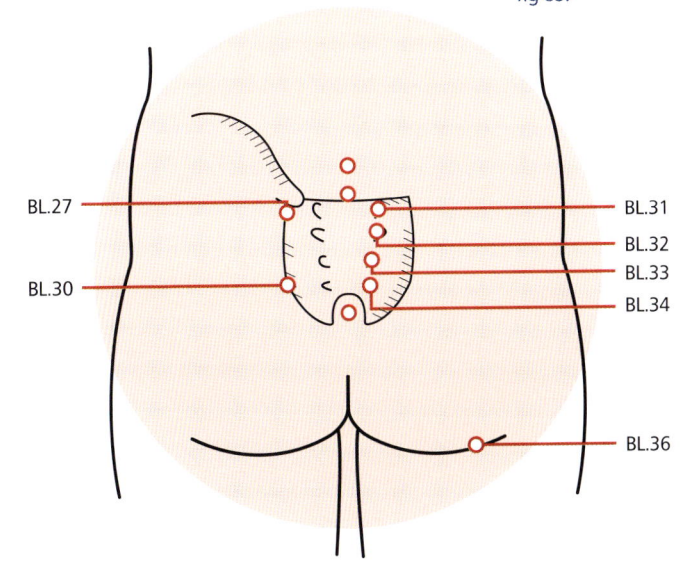

ACUPUNCTURE POINTS

BLADDER 35

Location: 0.5 cun lateral to the posterior midline level with the tip of the coccyx (fig 84).

Needling: Perpendicular insertion 1.0-1.5 cun

Uses: (i) Local point for coccygeal pain (ii) traditionally used to treat haemorrhoids and rectal prolapse (iii) The area must be cleaned thoroughly with an antiseptic wipe prior to needle insertion.

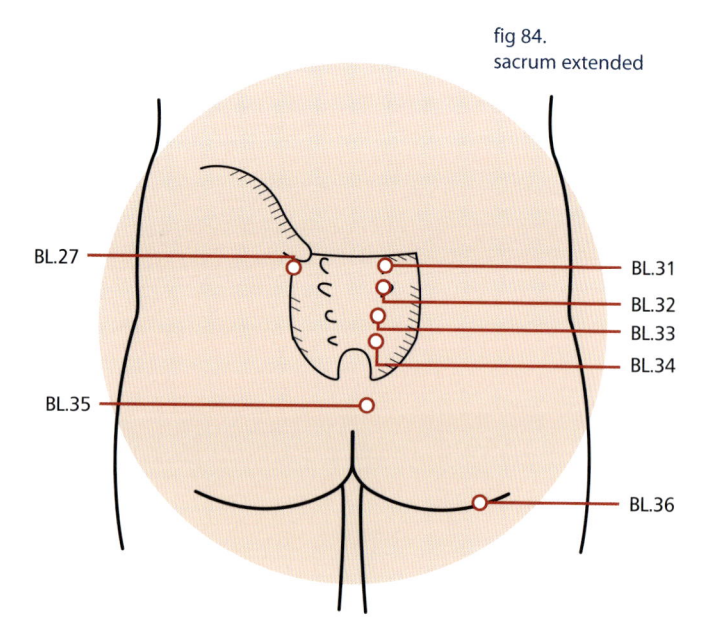

fig 84.
sacrum extended

BL.27
BL.31
BL.32
BL.33
BL.34
BL.35
BL.36

ACUPUNCTURE POINTS

BLADDER 36

Location: Just below the buttock, in the centre of the inferior (transverse) gluteal crease. (fig 85)

Needling: Perpendicular insertion 1 to 1.5 cun

Uses: Sciatic pain radiating into the leg. Local point over the ischial tuberosity for hamstring insertion pain.

BLADDER 37

Location: On the back of the thigh, 6 cun distal to the inferior gluteal crease (BL-36). On a line connecting BL-36 and BL-40 (fig 85).

Needling: Perpendicular insertion 1 to 2 cun

Uses: Local point for sciatic and mid belly hamstring pain.

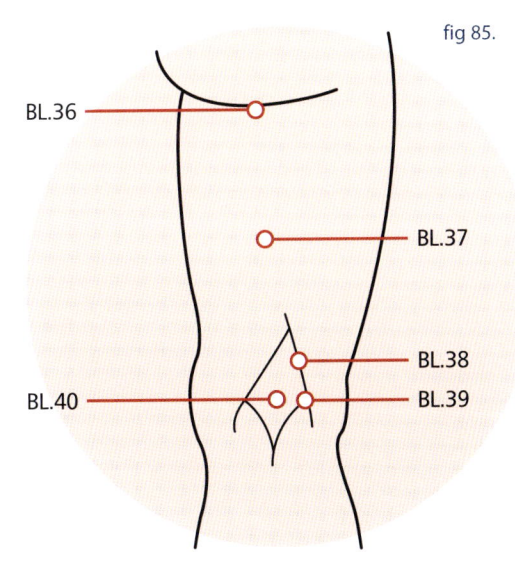

fig 85.

ACUPUNCTURE POINTS

BLADDER 38

Location: 1 cun superior to BL-39 on the medial aspect of the Biceps femoris tendon (fig 86)

Needling: Perpendicular insertion 1.0-1.5 cun

Uses: Local point for pain at the biceps tendon and postero-lateral knee pain

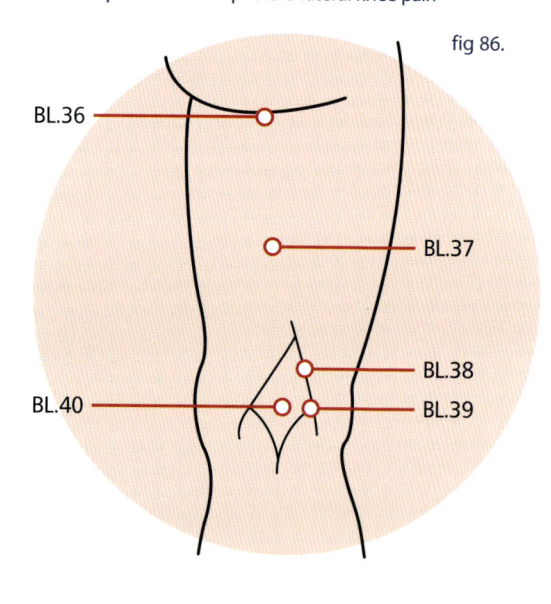

fig 86.

ACUPUNCTURE POINTS

BLADDER 39
Location: On the transverse popliteal crease, lateral to BL-40. In the depression medial to the biceps femoris muscle (fig 87).

Needling: Perpendicular insertion 0.5 – 1.0 cun

Note: This point lies close to the common peroneal nerve

Uses: (i) Local point for pain at the biceps tendon and postero-lateral knee pain (ii) lower *He-Sea point* of the triple energiser channel.

BLADDER 40
Location: At the midpoint of the popliteal crease of the knee, midway between the tendons of biceps femoris and semitendinosus (fig 87).

Needling: Perpendicular insertion 0.5 – 1.0 cun.

Note: This point lies over the popliteal artery and tibial nerve.

Uses: Sciatic pain referred into the knee (*heavenly star* point).

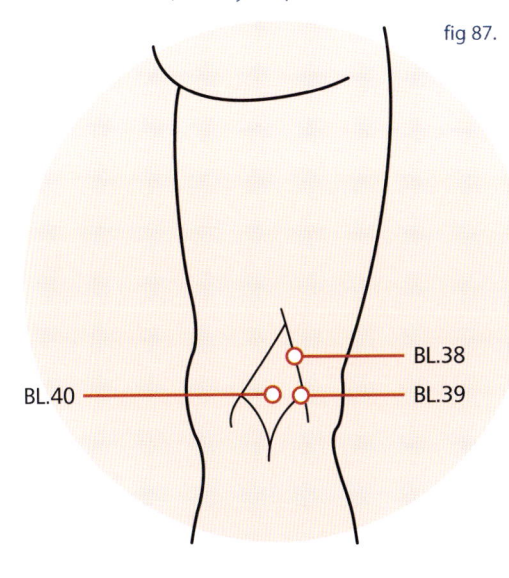

fig 87.

BL.38
BL.40
BL.39

ACUPUNCTURE POINTS

BLADDER 41-53

Location: 3 cun lateral to the midline, level with the lower border of the corresponding spinous process (fig 88).

Needling: Oblique insertion medial 0.3 to 0.5 cun.

Note: To aid surface marking, the following are approximate guidelines (i) The medial border of the scapula lies 3 cun lateral to the midline (ii) The inferior angle of the scapula lies at T7 (iii) The root of the scapular spine lies at T3 (iv) The spinous process of T12 is level with the midpoint of a vertical line between the inferior angle of the scapula and the iliac crest.

Uses: (i) used for local pain (ii) trigger points for the Erector Spinae (iliocostalis) and Rhomboid muscles (iii) Traditionally used for chronic conditions affecting the organs.

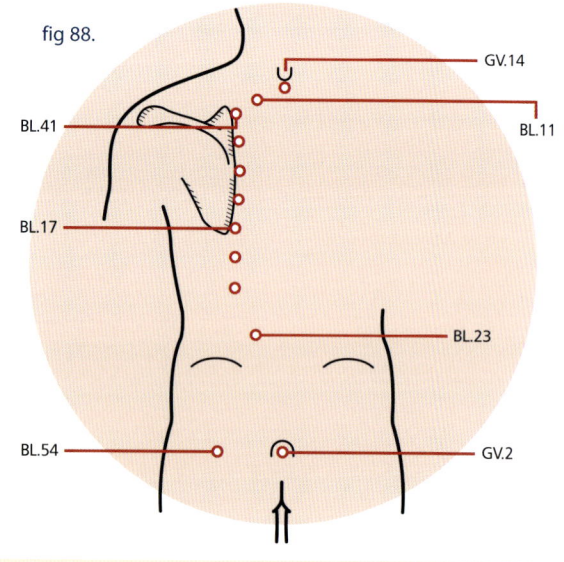

fig 88.

Point	Level	Area / organ	Point	Level	Shu
BL-41	T2	Upper scapula	BL-48	T10	GB / middle TE
BL-42	T3	LU	BL-49	T11	SP / ST / Middle TE
BL-43	T4	LU / HT / KI / SP / ST	BL-50	T12	Middle TE
BL-44	T5	Chest / upper TE	BL-51	L1	Breasts
BL-45	T6	LU / chest	BL-52	L2	KI / Lumbar
BL-46	T7	Diaphragm / middle TE	BL-53	S2	Lumbar / lower TE
BL-47	T9	LR / SP / ST / middle TE			

ACUPUNCTURE POINTS

BLADDER 54

Location: 3 cun lateral to the sacro-coccygeal hiatus (GV-2), at the level of the 4th sacral foramen (fig 89).

Needling: Perpendicular insertion 1.5 to 2.0 cun.

Note: This point is often a trigger point for the Piriformis muscle.

Uses: Sciatic pain referred into the buttock. Piriformis syndrome.

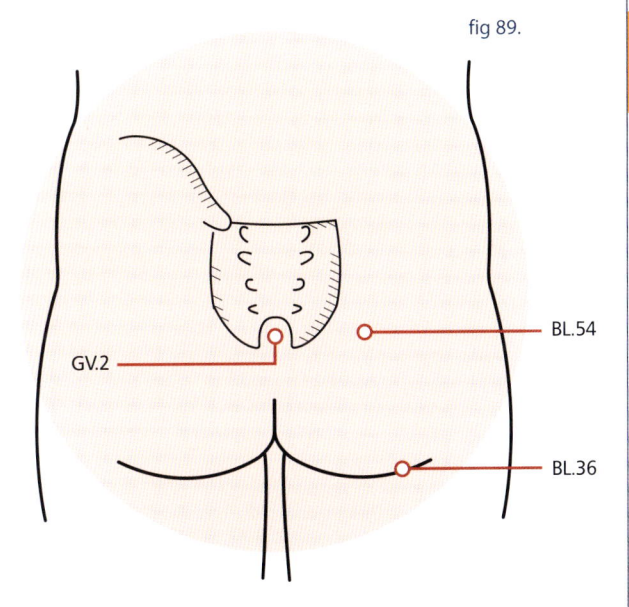

fig 89.

ACUPUNCTURE POINTS

BLADDER 55 / 56 / 57

Location: On a line from BL-40 through the medial and lateral bellies of the gastrocnemius muscle (fig 90)
- BL-55 lies 2 cun distal to BL-40.
- BL-56 lies 5 cun distal to BL-40.
- BL-57 lies midway between BL-40 and BL-60 (fig. 37).

Needling: Perpendicular insertion 0.8 – 1.2 cun.

Uses: (i) Local calf and posterior leg pain (ii) BL-57 is a *heavenly star* point for Sciatic pain referred into the calf.

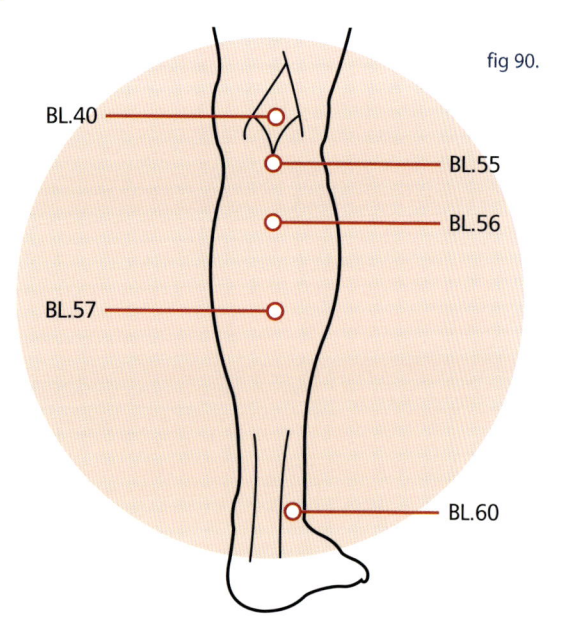

fig 90.

ACUPUNCTURE POINTS

BLADDER 58

Location: On the postero-lateral calf, 1 cun lateral and distal to Bl-57 (fig 91)

Needling: Perpendicular insertion 0.8 1.0 cun

Note: This point lies 7 cun proximal to BL-60 (level with the apex of the lateral malleolus).

Uses: (i) Local calf pain (ii) *Luo connecting point* of the bladder channel

BLADDER 59

Location: On the lateral aspect of the lower leg, 3 cun proximal to BL-60 (fig 91)

Needling: Perpendicular or oblique insertion 1-0-1.5 cun into the gap between the Achilles tendon and the peroneal muscles,.

Uses: (i) local pain in the Achilles tendon (ii) *Xi-cleft point* of the yang motility vessel

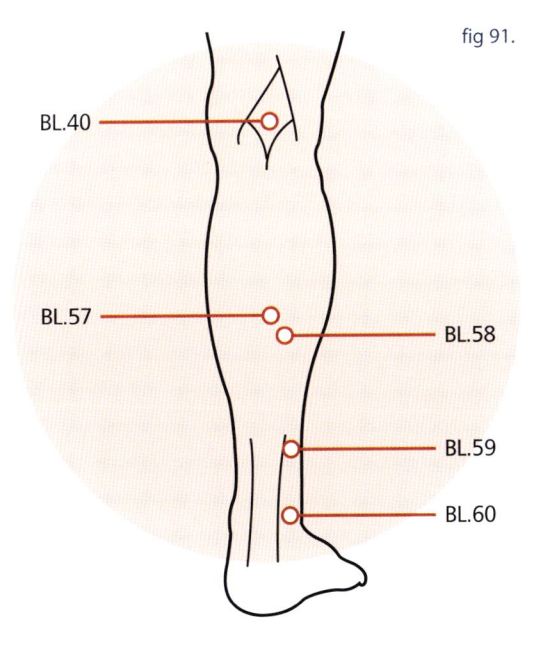

fig 91.

ACUPUNCTURE POINTS

BLADDER 60

Location: Between the apex of the lateral malleolus and the achilles tendon (Kager triangle) (fig 92)

Needling: Perpendicular insertion 0.5-0.8 cun

Note: This point is approximately opposite KI-3, which is similarly related to the apex of the medial malleolus. However, as the medial malleolus is higher than the lateral, the two points are not directly in line. This point is said to be contraindicated in pregnancy.

Uses: (i) Local point for achilles tendon conditions. (ii) *Heavenly star* point for Sciatica referred into the foot

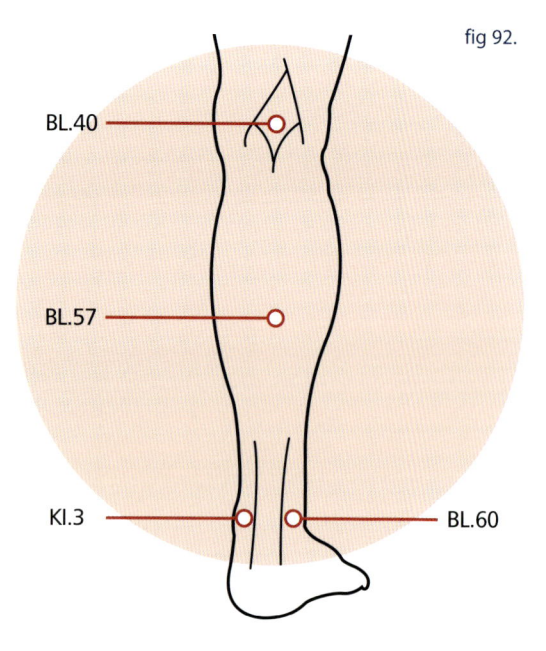

fig 92.

ACUPUNCTURE POINTS

BLADDER 61
Location: On the lateral aspect of the foot, 1.5 cun inferior to BL-60 (fig 93)

Needling: Transverse insertion 0.3-0.5 cun

Uses: (i) Local point for heel pain (ii) *Meeting point* of the Bladder channel and Yang motility vessel.

BLADDER 62
Location: In the depression at the inferior edge of the lateral malleolus (fig 93).

Needling: Oblique insertion 0.3 cun

Note: The point lies in line with the apex of the malleolus, slightly below and behind the peroneal tendons.

Uses: (i) Local point for heal pain, and lateral ankle pain. (ii) Traditionally used to treat headaches, and dizziness. (iii) *Confluence point* of the yang motility vessel.

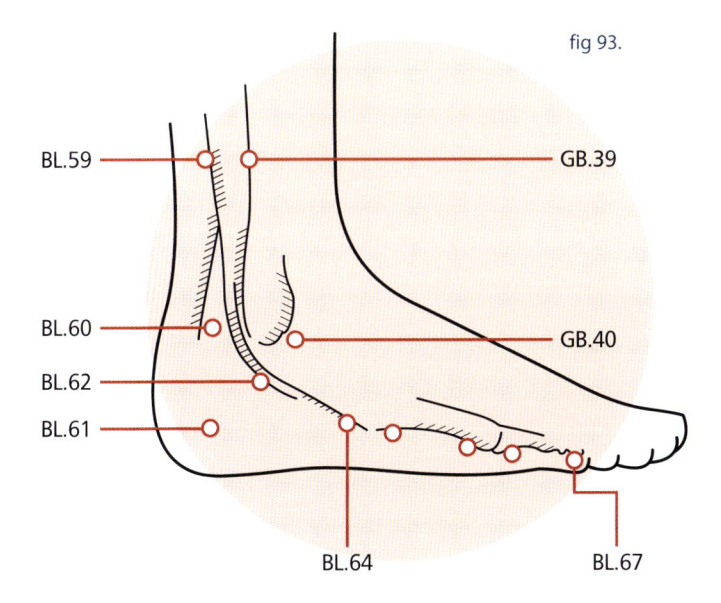

fig 93.

ACUPUNCTURE POINTS

BLADDER 63 / 64

Bladder 63 / 64
Location: On the lateral aspect of the foot (fig 94)
- BL-63 lies proximal to the tuberosity of the 5th metatarsal bone
- BL-64 lies distal to the tuberosity of the 5th metatarsal bone

Needling: perpendicular or oblique insertion 0.3-0.5 cun

Uses: (i) Lateral foot pain (ii) BL-63 is the *Xi-cleft point* of the bladder channel and the meeting point of the Bladder channel and yang linking vessel (iii) BL-64 is the *source point* of the bladder channel.

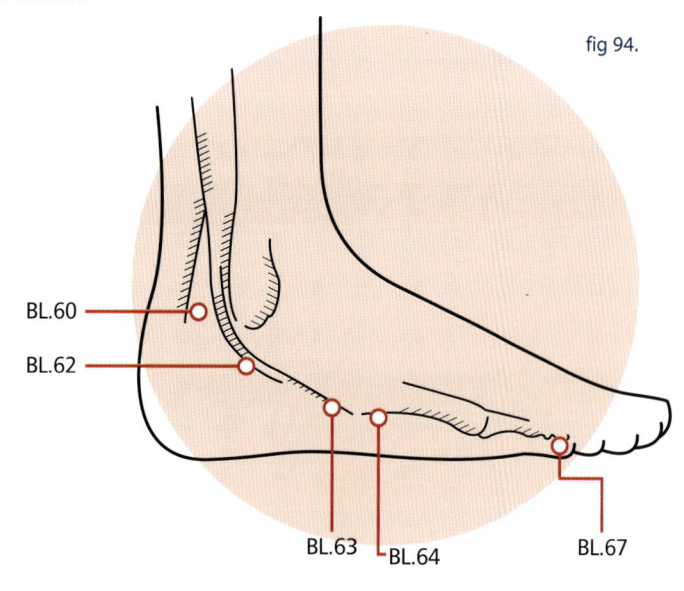

fig 94.

ACUPUNCTURE POINTS

BLADDER 65 / 66
Location: On the lateral aspect of the foot (fig 95)
- BL-65 lies proximal to the head of the 5th metatarsal,
- BL-65 distal to the metatarsal phalangeal (MTP) joint

Needling: Perpendicular or oblique 0.3 – 0.5 cun

Uses: Lateral foot and toe pain.

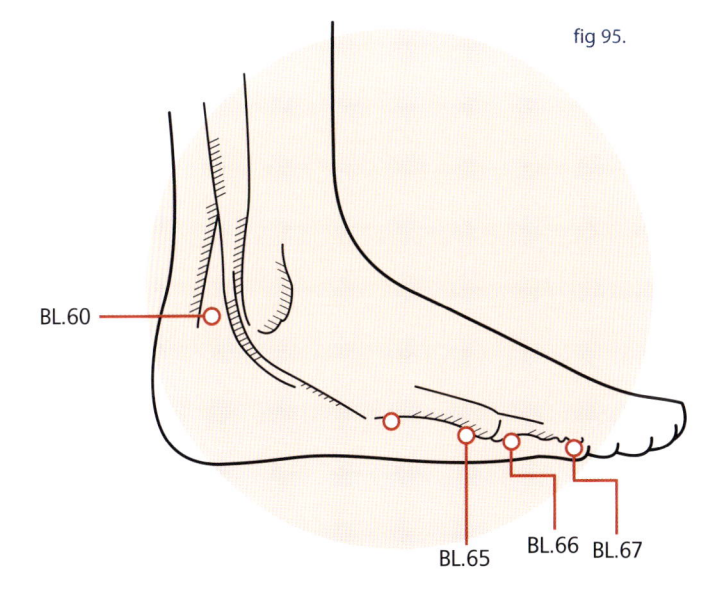

fig 95.

ACUPUNCTURE POINTS

BLADDER 67

Location: On the dorsal aspect of the little toe at the lateral nail point. (fig 96).

Needling: Perpendicular insertion 0.1 to 0.2 cun.

Uses: (i) Said to benefit the eyes. (ii) Traditionally used for headache and malposition of the foetus.

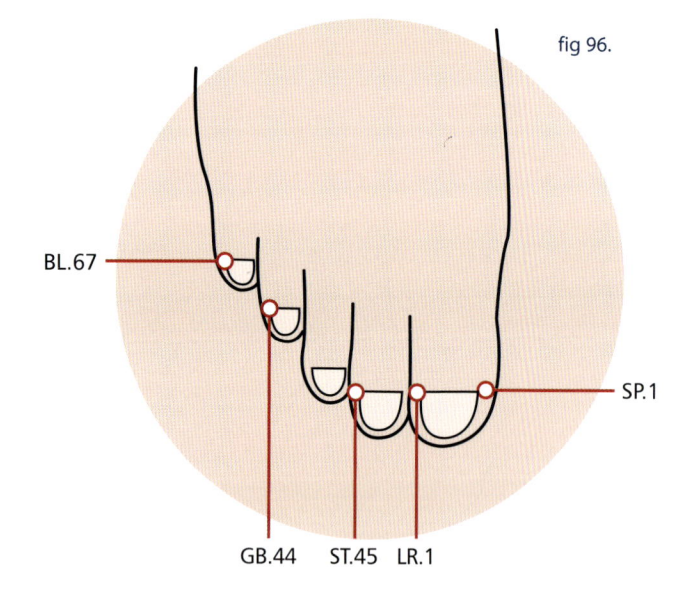

fig 96.

BL.67

SP.1

GB.44   ST.45   LR.1

ACUPUNCTURE POINTS

KIDNEY (KI)

KIDNEY 1

Location: On the sole of the foot, 1/3rd of the distance between the base of the 2nd toe and the heel. The point is located between the 2nd and 3rd metatarsal bones (fig 97).

Needling: Perpendicular insertion 0.5 to 1 cun. The point is more comfortable to acupressure.

Note: This point lies in the depression formed when the foot is plantar flexed.

Uses: (i) Local point for plantar fascial pain. (ii) Traditionally used to treat headache, dizziness, and loss of voice.

fig 97.

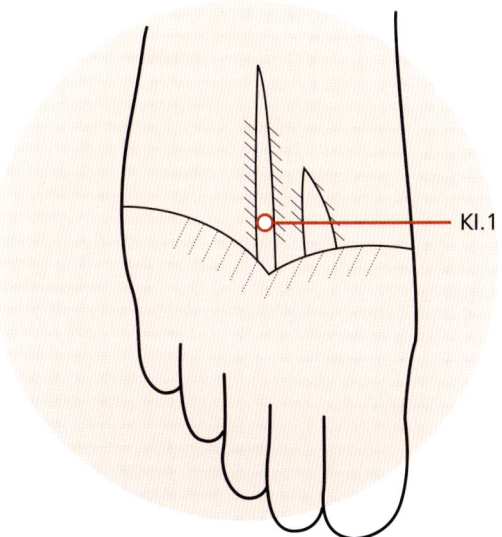

KI.1

ACUPUNCTURE POINTS

KIDNEY 2

Location: On the medial aspect of the foot, distal and inferior to the tubercle of the Navicular bone (fig 98).

Needling: Perpendicular insertion 0.5-1.0 cun

Uses: Local medial arch pain,

KIDNEY 3

Location: In the centre of the depression between the apex of the medial malleolus and the Achilles tendon (Kager's triangle) (fig 98).

Needling: Perpendicular insertion 0.5 to 1 cun.

Note: This point is approximately opposite BL-60, which is similarly related to the apex of the lateral malleolus. However, as the medial malleolus is higher than the lateral, the two points are not directly opposite.

Uses: (i) Achilles tendon pain. (ii) Often used point to treat headaches. (iii) *Source point* of the Kidney channel.

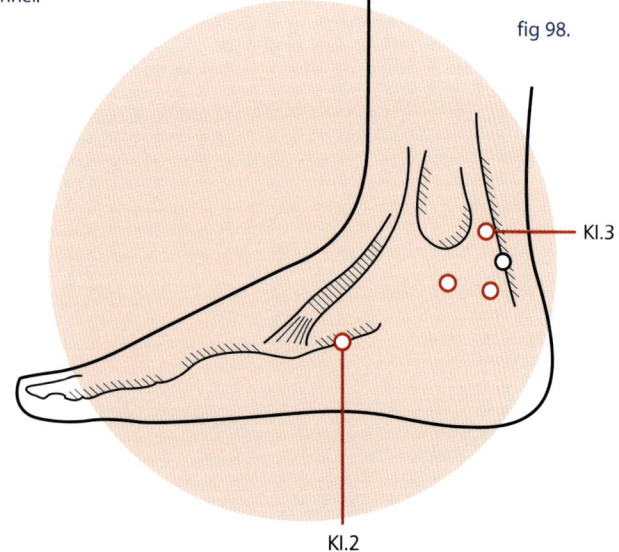

fig 98.

ACUPUNCTURE POINTS

KIDNEY 4

Location: On the medial aspect of the rear foot, anterior and superior to the Achilles tendon insertion onto the Calcaneus (fig 99)

Needling: Perpendicular 0.3-0.5 cun

Note: This point lies at the midpoint of a line joining KI-3 and KI-5.

Uses: (i) local point for medial Achilles pain (ii) *Luo-connecting point* of the Kidney channel.

KIDNEY 5

Location: 1 cun distal to KI-3 in the depression posterior to the talo-calcaneal joint (fig 99).

Needling: Oblique insertion 0.3-0.5 cun

Uses: (i) Local point for Achilles pain (ii) *Xi-cleft point* of the Kidney channel.

KIDNEY 6

Location: 1 cun below the apex of the medial malleolus. The point lies between the two bundles of the medial (Deltoid) ligament of the ankle (fig 99).

Needling: Oblique insertion directed superiorly 0.3 to 0.5 cun

Note: KI-6 is located between the tendons of tibialis posterior and flexor digitorum longus.

Uses: (i) Local point for medial ligament sprain of the ankle.
(ii) *Confluence point* of the Yin motility vessel
(iii) traditionally used to treat throat disorders and to *nourish* the Kidney.

fig 99.

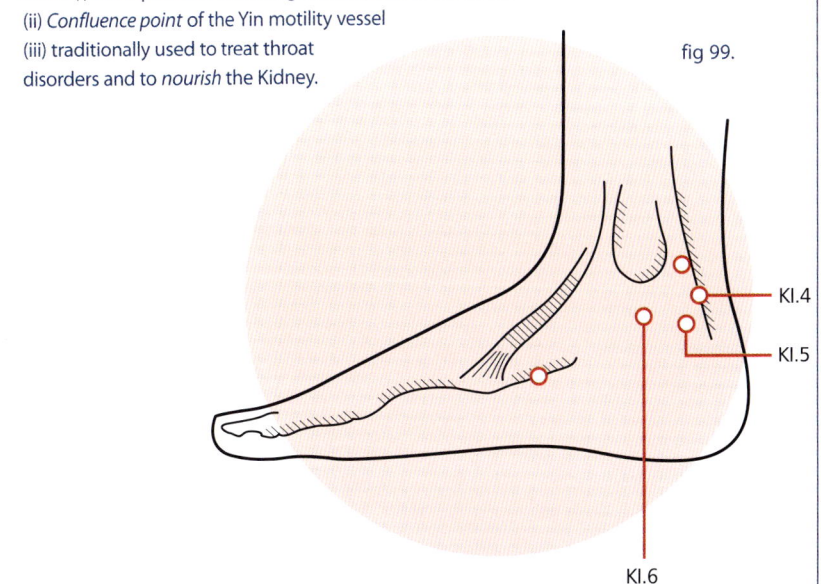

ACUPUNCTURE POINTS

KIDNEY 7/8

Location: on the medial aspect of the shin (fig 100)
- KI-7 lies 2 cun superior to KI-3.
- KI-8 lies 0.5 anterior to KI-7

Needling: Perpendicular insertion 0.5-1.0 cun

Uses: (i) local points for Achilles tendon pain (ii) KI-8 is the *Xi-cleft* point of the Yin motility vessel (iii) KI-8 is used traditionally to regulate menstruation.

KIDNEY 9

Location: On the medial aspect of the lower leg, 5 cun superior to KI-3 (fig 100).

Needling: Perpendicular insertion 1.0-1.5 cun

Uses: (i) Local point for lower medial calf pain (ii) traditionally used to *transform phlegm* (iii) *Xi-cleft point* of the yin linking vessel.

KIDNEY 10

Location: At the medial end of the popliteal crease, between the tendons of semitendinosus and semimembranosus (fig 100).

Needling: Perpendicular insertion 1 to 1.5 cun

Note: The point is more easily located with the knee slightly flexed.

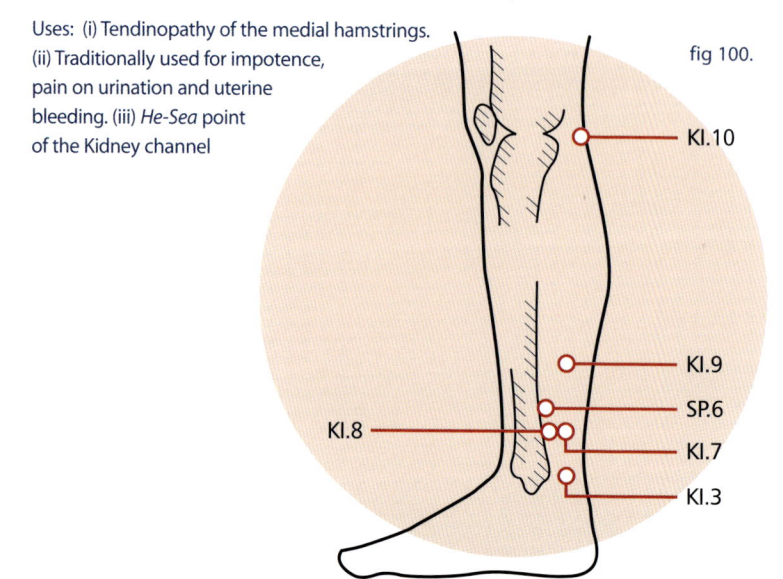

Uses: (i) Tendinopathy of the medial hamstrings. (ii) Traditionally used for impotence, pain on urination and uterine bleeding. (iii) *He-Sea* point of the Kidney channel

fig 100.

ACUPUNCTURE POINTS

KIDNEY 11 - 21

Location: Each point lies 0.5 cun from the midline, at a distance from the superior border of the symphysis pubis (KI-11 to 15) (fig 101) or above the umbilicus (KI-16 to 21) (fig 102).

KI-11............ at the symphysis,	KI-16............level with the umbilicus
KI-12............ 1 cun above	KI-17............2 cun above
KI-13............ 2 cun above	KI-18............3 cun above
KI-14............ 3 cun above	KI-19............4 cun above
KI-15............ 4 cun above	KI-20............5 cun above
	KI-21............6 cun above

Needling: 0.5 – 1.0 cun perpendicular

Note: Lower Kidney points should be used with caution in pregnancy. They should be needled with the bladder empty.

Uses: (i) Local points for strain of the rectus abdominis muscle. (ii) Traditionally used to *harmonise* the internal organs. (iii) *meeting points* of the kidney channel with the penetrating vessel.

fig 101.

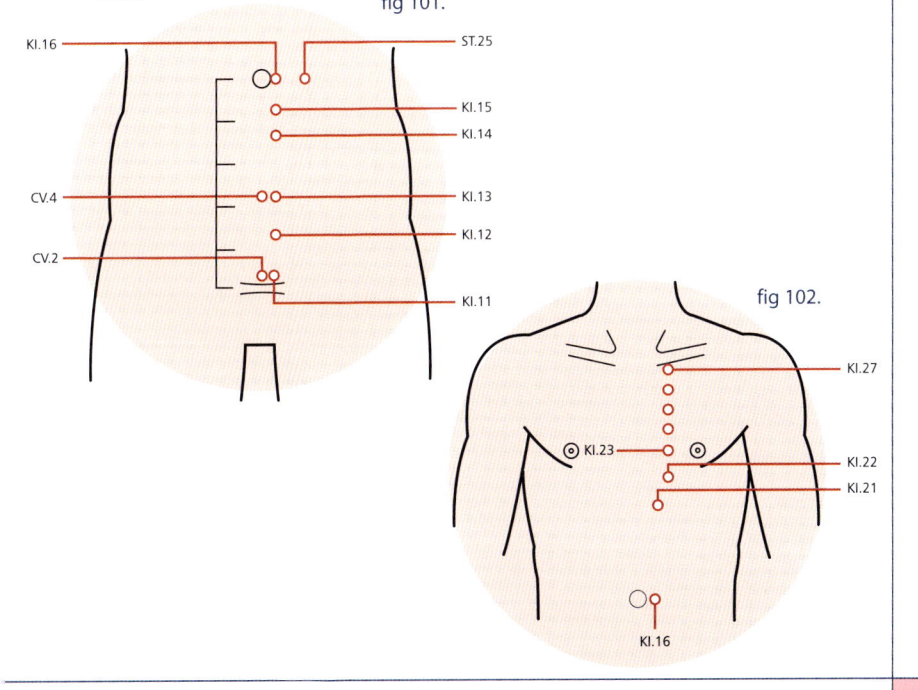

fig 102.

ACUPUNCTURE POINTS

KIDNEY 22-26

Location: Each point lies 2 cun lateral to the midline, within the intercostal spaces (fig 103).
- KI-22 within the 5th intercostal space
- KI-23 within the 4th intercostal space
- KI-24 within the 3rd intercostal space
- KI-25 within the 2nd intercostal space
- KI-26 within the 1st intercostal space

Needling: 0.5-1.0 cun perpendicular or oblique

Note: Deep needling may cause pneumothorax

Uses: (i) local points for intercostal pain (ii) traditionally used to *unbind the chest* in cases of cough and dyspnoea.

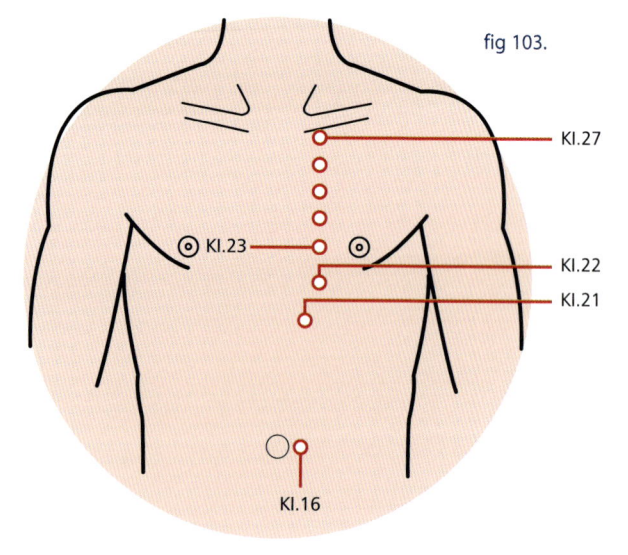

fig 103.

ACUPUNCTURE POINTS

KIDNEY 27

Location: 2 cun lateral to the midline in the depression at the lower border of the clavicle (fig 40)
Needling: Transverse or oblique insertion 0.5-0.8 cun
Uses: (i) traditionally used to *unbind the chest* and alleviate cough and wheezing.

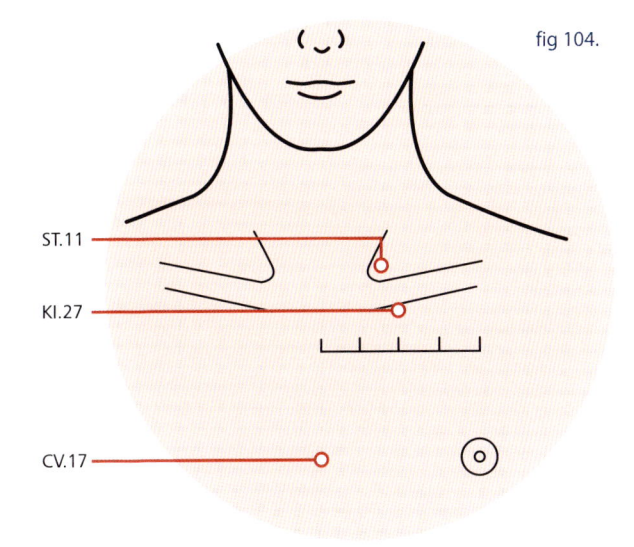

fig 104.

ST.11
KI.27
CV.17

ACUPUNCTURE POINTS

PERICARDIUM (PC)

PERICARDIUM 1

Location: 1 cun lateral to the nipple in the 4th intercostals space (fig 105)

Needling: Transverse insertion 0.5 cun

Uses: (i) Traditionally used to *unbind the chest* and treat the breast

fig 105.

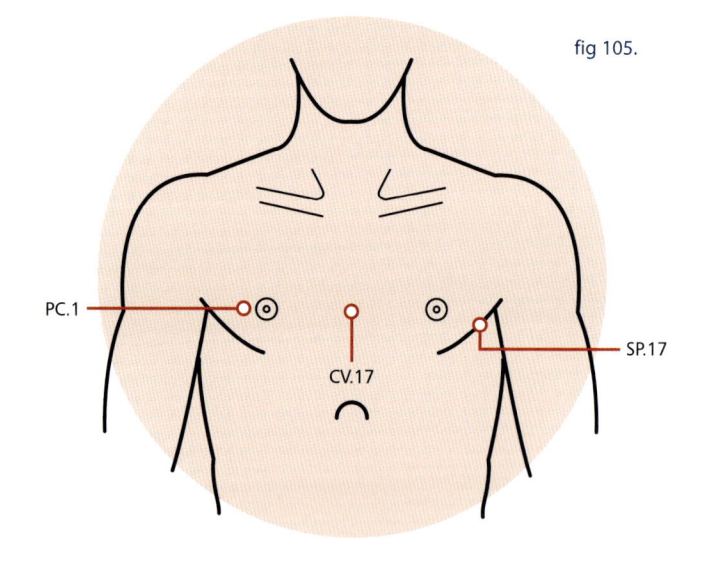

ACUPUNCTURE POINTS

PERICARDIUM 2

Location: On the anterior aspect of the arm between the two heads of the biceps brachii muscle. The point lies 2 cun below the anterior axillary fold (fig 106)

Needling: Oblique insertion 1.0-1.5 cun along the line of the channel

Uses: (i) Local point for biceps pain (ii) traditionally used to treat heart and chest pain.

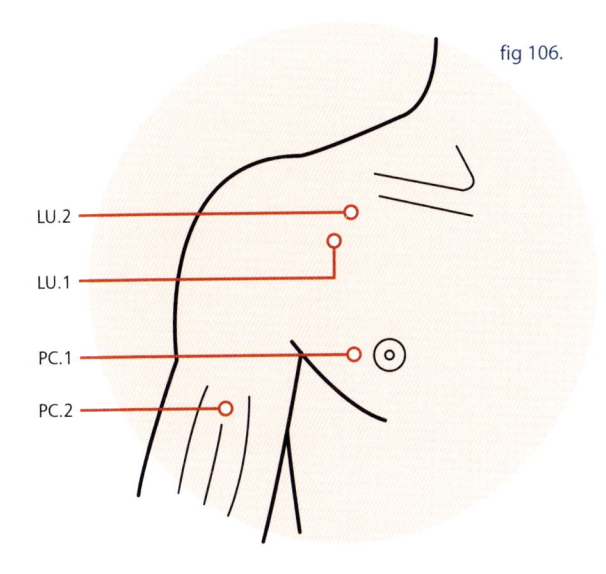

fig 106.

ACUPUNCTURE POINTS

PERICARDIUM 3

Location: On the transverse cubital crease, to the ulnar side of the biceps tendon. Locate with the elbow slightly flexed (fig 107).

Needling: Perpendicular insertion 0.5 to 1 cun

Uses: (i) Local point for biceps tendon pain, and conditions of the elbow joint. (ii) Traditionally used for angina and palpitations, and to *drain heat*.

PERICARDIUM 4

Location: On the flexor aspect of the forearm, 5 cun proximal to the wrist crease (PC-7) (fig 107).

Needling: Perpendicular insertion 0.5 to 1 cun or oblique insertion up to 1.5 cun

Note: This points lies between the tendons of palmaris longus and flexor carpi radialis.

Uses: (i) Traditionally used to treat acute chest pain radiating to the neck. (ii) *Xi-cleft* point of the Pericardium channel.

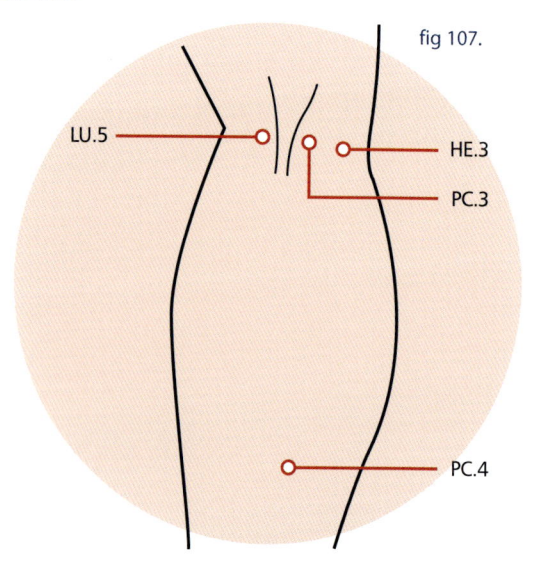

fig 107.

ACUPUNCTURE POINTS

PERICARDIUM 5
Location: On the flexor aspect of the forearm, 3 cun proximal to the wrist crease (PC-7) (fig 108).

Needling: Perpendicular insertion 0.5 to 1 cun or oblique insertion up to 1.5 cun

Note: This points lies between the tendons of palmaris longus and flexor carpi radialis.

Uses: (i) Traditionally used to treat restlessness and palpitations. (ii) May be used in epilepsy.

PERICARDIUM 6
Location: On the flexor aspect of the forearm, 2 cun proximal to the wrist crease (PC-7) (fig 108).

Needling: Perpendicular insertion 0.5 to 1 cun or oblique insertion up to 1.5 cun.

Note: This points lies between the tendons of palmaris longus and flexor carpi radialis.

Uses: (i) Much used point to treat nausea and vomiting. (ii) *Luo-connecting point* of the Pericardium channel. *Confluence point* of the Yin linking vessel.

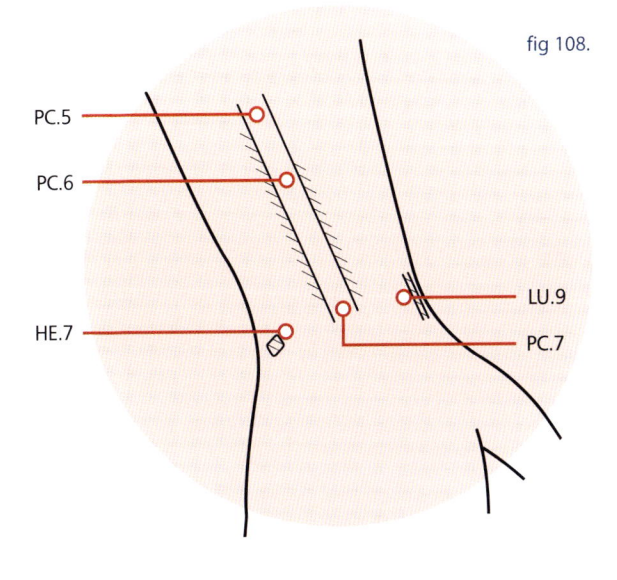

fig 108.

PC.5
PC.6
HE.7
LU.9
PC.7

ACUPUNCTURE POINTS

PERICARDIUM 7

Location: At the wrist between the tendons of palmaris longus and flexor carpi radialis (fig 109).

Needling: Perpendicular insertion 0.3 to 0.5 cun, or oblique distal insertion along the carpal tunnel.

Note: the median nerve lies directly under this point and deep needling / manipulation may damage the nerve

Uses: (i) Local point to treat wrist pain and carpal tunnel disorder. (ii) May also be used to treat angina. (iii) *Source point* of the pericardium channel.

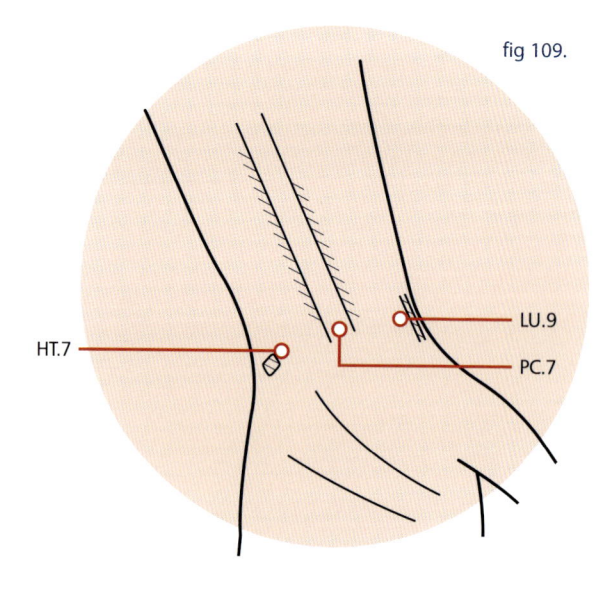

fig 109.

ACUPUNCTURE POINTS

PERICARDIUM 8
Location: In the centre of the palm between the 2nd and 3rd metacarpals, proximal to the metacarpophalangeal (MCP) joint (fig 110).

Needling: Perpendicular insertion 0.5 cun

Note: This point lies where the tip of the middle finger touches the palm when a fist is made.

Uses: Local point for palm pain and contraction.

fig 110.

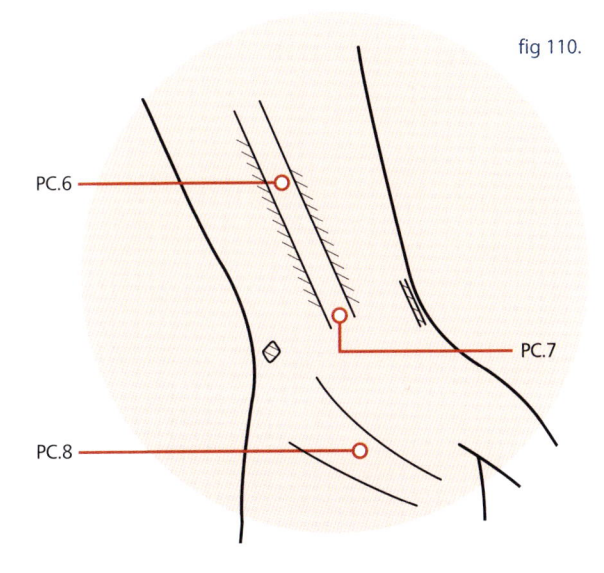

ACUPUNCTURE POINTS

PERICARDIUM 9

Location: On the radial nail point of the middle finger (fig 111).

Needling: Perpendicular insertion 0.1 to 0.2 cun.

Uses: Said to treat loss of consciousness.

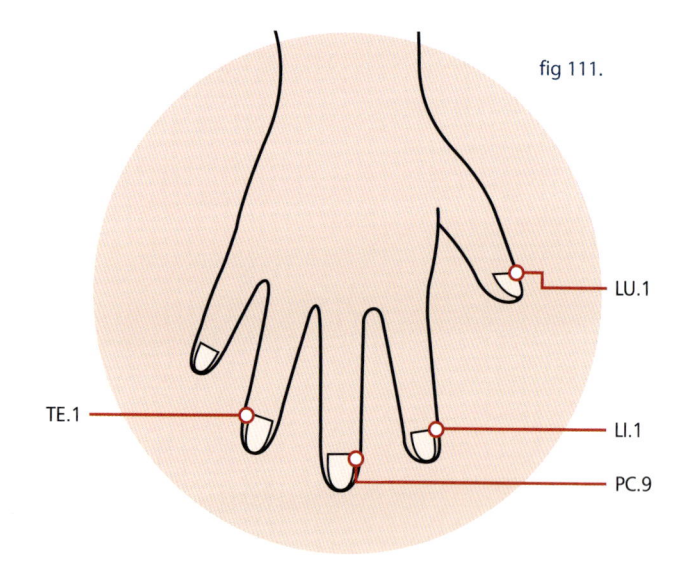

fig 111.

TE.1

LU.1

LI.1

PC.9

ACUPUNCTURE POINTS

TRIPLE ENERGISER (TE)

TRIPLE ENERGISER 1

Location: The ulnar nail point of the 4th finger (fig 112).

Needling: Perpendicular insertion 0.1-0.2 cun

Uses: (i) Traditionally used for acute symptoms (ii) Claimed to *clear heat* from the channel.

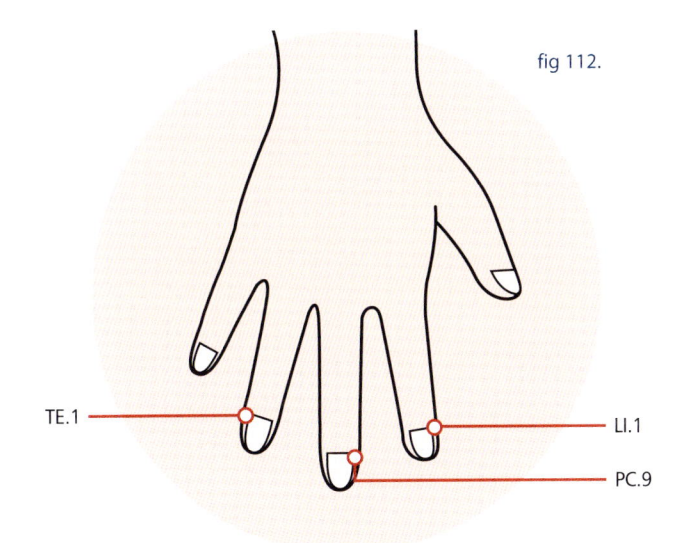

fig 112.

TE.1

LI.1

PC.9

ACUPUNCTURE POINTS

TRIPLE ENERGISER 2 / 3

Location: On the dorsum of the hand, between the 4th and 5th fingers.
- TE-2 lies in the depression distal to the metacarpophalangeal (MCP) joint
- TE-3 lies proximal to the MCP joint (fig 113)

Needling: Perpendicular or oblique insertion 0.5 to 1 cun.

Note: TE-2 lies just proximal to the edge of the finger web

Uses: (i) Local points for pain in the upper ulnar aspect of the hand. (ii) traditionally used to treat ear disorders and one sided headache.

TRIPLE ENERGISER 4

Location: On the dorsum of the wrist, at the level of the wrist joint. The point lies in a depression between the tendons of extensor digitorum communis and extensor digiti minimi (fig 113).

Needling: Perpendicular insertion 0.3 to 0.5 cun.

Note: To locate the point slide the palpating finger along the channel between the 4th and 5th finger until it reaches the depression at the wrist crease.

Uses: (i) Local point for dorsal wrist pain. (ii) *Source point* of the triple energiser channel.

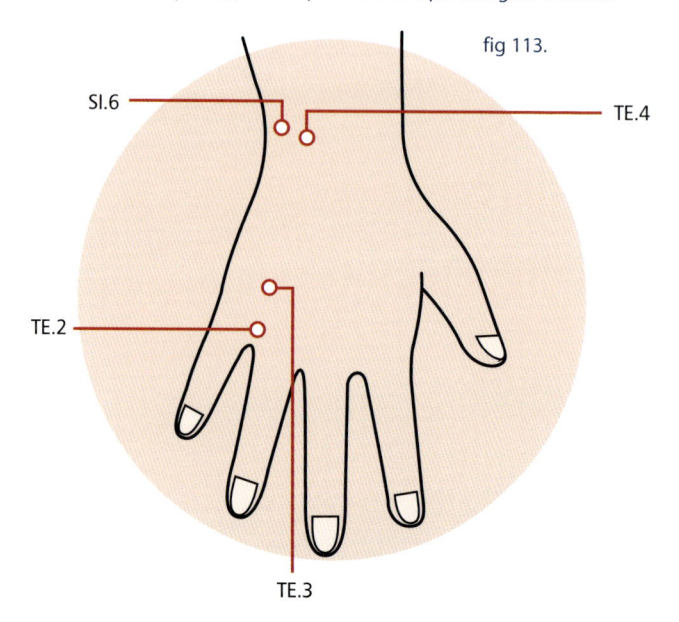

fig 113.

ACUPUNCTURE POINTS

TRIPLE ENERGISER 5

Location: 2 cun proximal to the dorsal wrist crease (TE-4) in the depression between the radius and the ulna (fig 114).

Needling: Perpendicular insertion 0.5 – 1.0 cun

Note: This point is directly opposite PC-6

Uses: (i) Pain / inflammation of the ear and eye. (ii) Posterior shoulder and arm pain. (iii) *Luo-connecting* point of the Triple Energiser channel and *confluence point* of the Yang Linking Vessel.

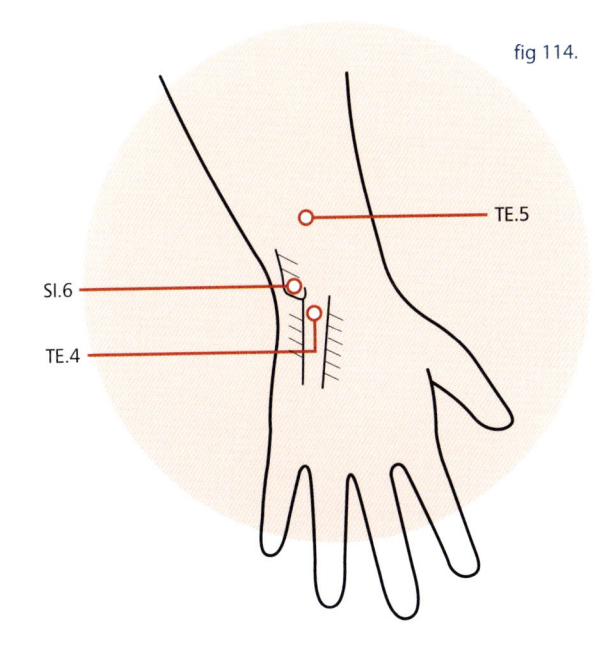

fig 114.

ACUPUNCTURE POINTS

TRIPLE ENERGISER 6

Location: 3 cun proximal to the dorsal wrist crease, between the radius and ulna. The point lies 1 cun proximal to TE-5 (fig 115).

Needling: 0.8 – 1.2 cun perpendicular.

Uses: Acute shoulder and arm pain. May be used for intercostal neuralgia.

fig 115.

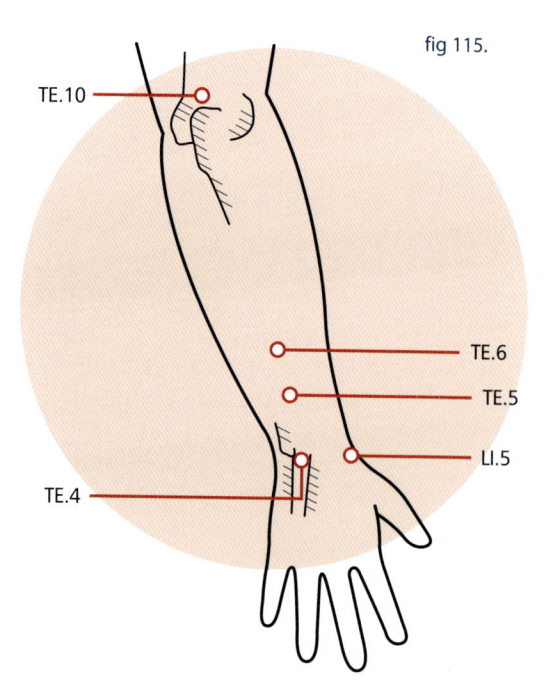

ACUPUNCTURE POINTS

TRIPLE ENERGISER 7 / 8 / 9

Location: Each point lies in the depression between the radius and ulna (fig 116)
- TE-7 lies 3 cun proximal to the wrist crease, on the ulnar side of TE.6
- TE-8 lies 4 cun proximal to the wrist crease
- TE-9 lies 7 cun proximal to the wrist crease

Needling: Perpendicular insertion 0.5-1.5 cun

Uses: (i) Pain in the forearm extensor muscles (ii) traditionally said to benefit the throat and ears. (iii) TE-7 is the *Xi-cleft* point of the Triple Energiser channel.

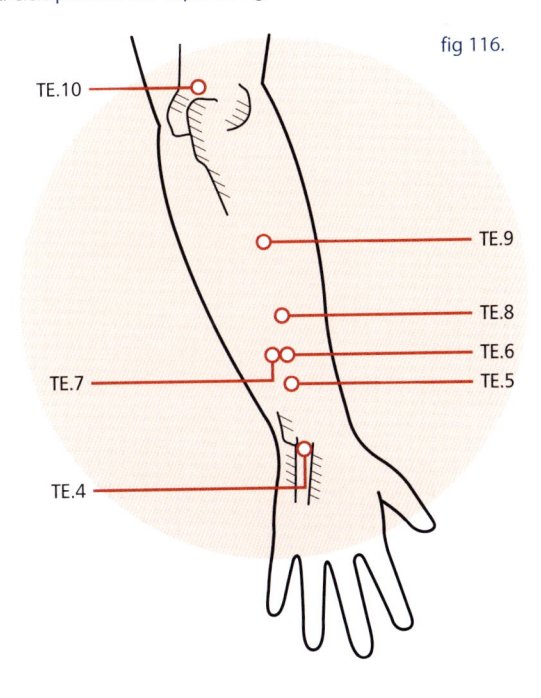

fig 116.

ACUPUNCTURE POINTS

TRIPLE ENERGISER 10

Location: With the elbow flexed, the point lies in a depression 1 cun proximal to the olecranon process (fig 117).

Needling: Perpendicular insertion 0.5 to 1 cun

Uses: (i) Local point for posterior elbow pain. (ii) Traditionally used to *transform phlegm and dissipate accumulation* (iii) Used in the treatment of neck and axillary nodules.

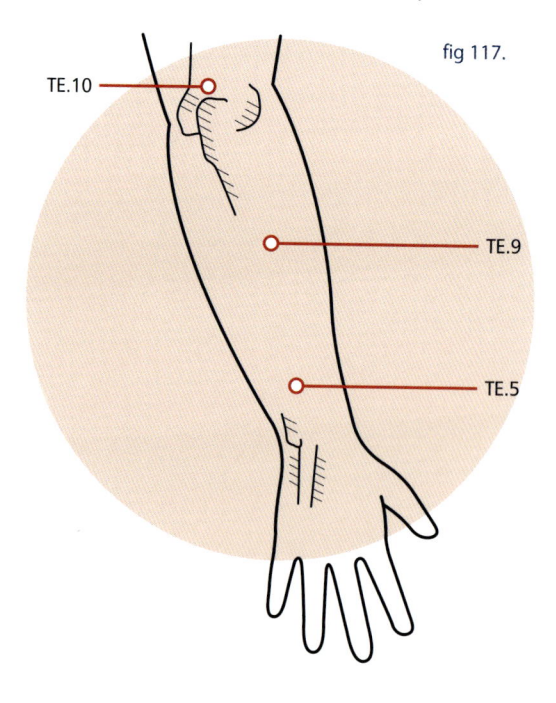

fig 117.

ACUPUNCTURE POINTS

TRIPLE ENERGISER 11 / 12 / 13

Location: On a line joining TE-10 and TE-14 (fig 118), the points lie as follows:
- TE-11 lies 1 cun proximal to TE-10,
- TE-12 lies 4 cun proximal to TE-10
- TE-13 lies 3 cun distal to TE-14.

Needling: Perpendicular insertion 1.0-1.5 cun

Note: TE-13 lies at the point where the line joining TE-10 and TE-14 meets the posterior deltoid muscle.

Uses: (i) Local points for posterior arm and triceps muscle pain. (ii) TE-13 is a *meeting point* of the Triple Energiser channel and Yang Linking vessel.

fig 118.

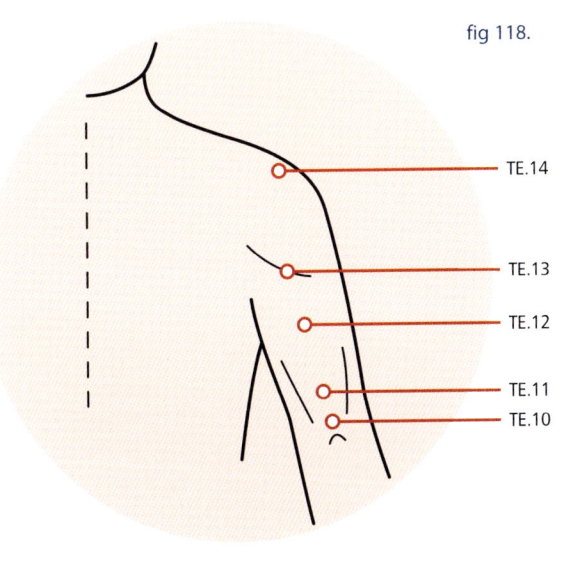

ACUPUNCTURE POINTS

TRIPLE ENERGISER 14

Location: In the depression distal to the posterior aspect of the acromion process (fig 119).

Needling: 1 – 1.5 cun perpendicular, directed towards the centre of the joint.

Note: This point is the posterior 'eye' of the shoulder, the anterior being LI-15.

Uses: Local point for posterior shoulder pain.

fig 119.

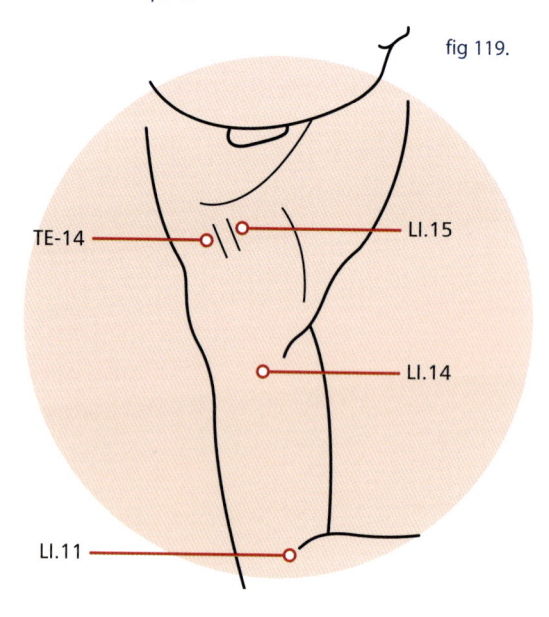

ACUPUNCTURE POINTS

TRIPLE ENERGISER 15

Location: Within the upper portion of the Suprascapular fossa, at the midpoint of a line joining C7 and the tip of the Acromion process (fig 120).

Needling: Oblique insertion 0.5-1.0 cun

Note: (i) deep perpendicular needling risks pneumothorax (ii) TE-15 may also be located at the midpoint of a line joining GB-21 and SI-13.

fig 120.

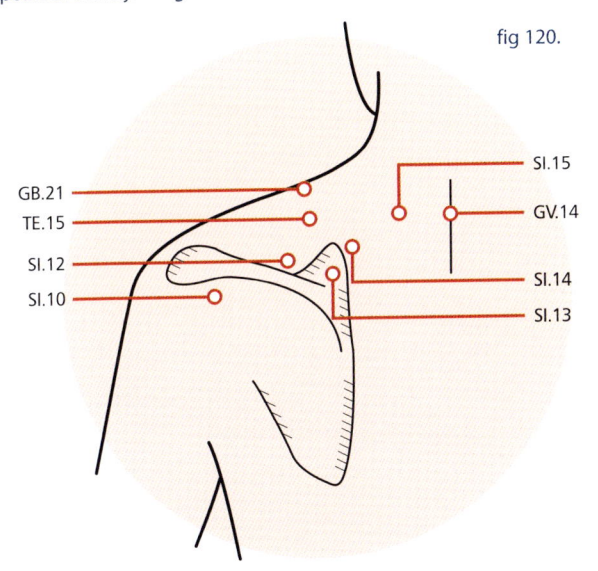

ACUPUNCTURE POINTS

TRIPLE ENERGISER 16

Location: Inferior to the Mastoid process on the posterior border of the Sternocleido-mastoid muscle. The point lies at the same level as the angle of the Mandible (fig 121).

Needling: Perpendicular or oblique insertion 0.5-1.0 cun

Note: (i) This point lies close to the Carotid artery (ii) TE-16 lies 1 cun below GB-12

Uses: (i) Traditionally used to benefit the head and sense organs (ii) *window of heaven* point.

fig 121.

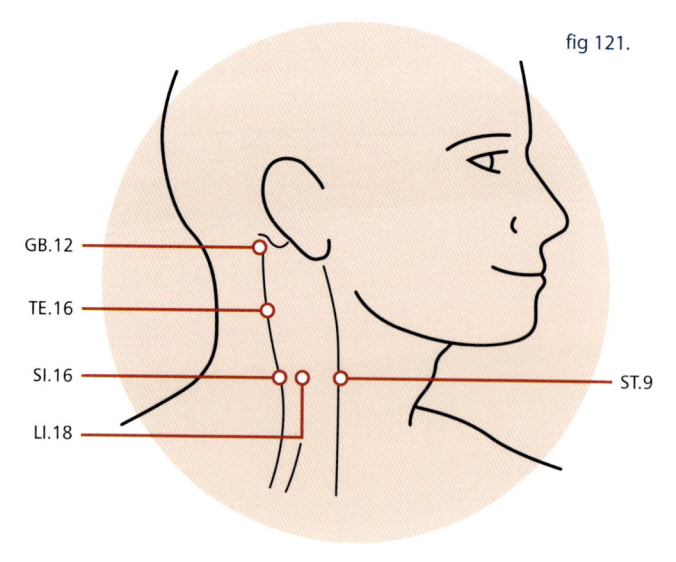

ACUPUNCTURE POINTS

TRIPLE ENERGISER 17

Location: Behind the earlobe, between the ramus of the mandible and the mastoid process (fig 122).

Needling: Perpendicular insertion, directed towards the opposite ear, 0.5 to 1 cun.

Note: Deep needling may damage the facial nerve

Uses: (i) Local point for tinnitus and facial paralysis especially when due to *pathogenic wind invasion.* (ii) *meeting point* of the Triple Energiser and Gall Bladder channels

fig 122.

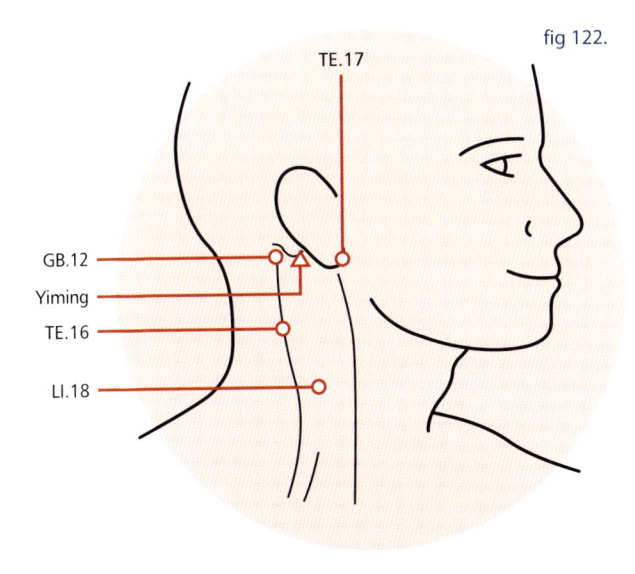

ACUPUNCTURE POINTS

TRIPLE ENERGISER 18 / 19 / 20

Location: On the side of the head each point lies on the meridian line around the ear from TE-17 (inferior) to TE-20 (superior) (fig 123).
- TE-18 lies 1/3rd of the distance along the line.
- TE-19 lies 2/3rd of the distance along the line
- TE-20 lies directly level with the apex of the ear

Needling: Transverse insertion 0.5 cun .

Uses: (i) Local points for one sided headache, tinnitus and ear pain. (ii) TE-20 is a *meeting point* of the Triple Energiser, Small Intestine and Gall Bladder channels

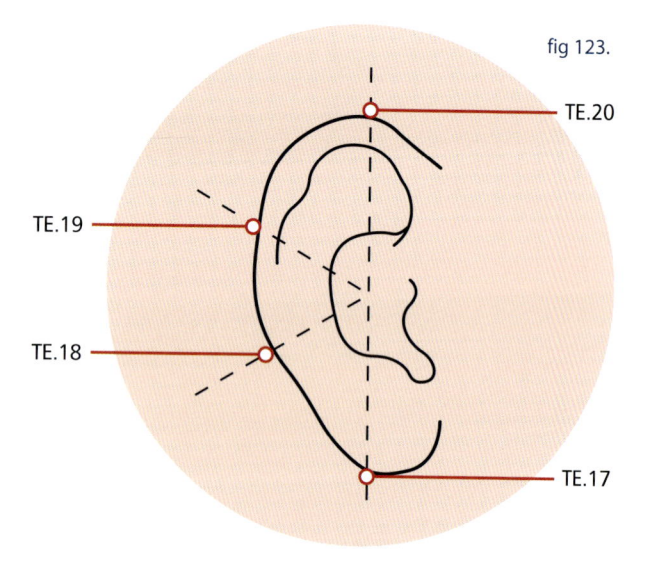

fig 123.

ACUPUNCTURE POINTS

TRIPLE ENERGISER 21

Location: In the depression anterior to the supratragic notch and superior to the condyloid process of the mandible (fig 124).

Needling: Inferior oblique insertion, 0.5 to 1 cun

Uses: Local point for ear pain.

fig 124.

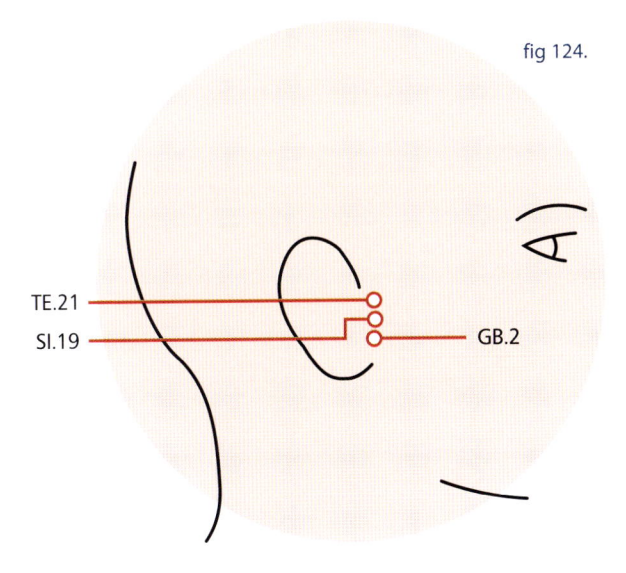

ACUPUNCTURE POINTS

TRIPLE ENERGISER 22

Location: Superior and anterior to TE-21, at the level of the upper border of the root of the ear (fig 125).

Needling: Transverse insertion 0.3-0.5 cun

Uses: (i) local point for tinnitus and ear pain (ii) *meeting point* of the Triple energiser, Small intestine and Gall Bladder channels.

fig 125.

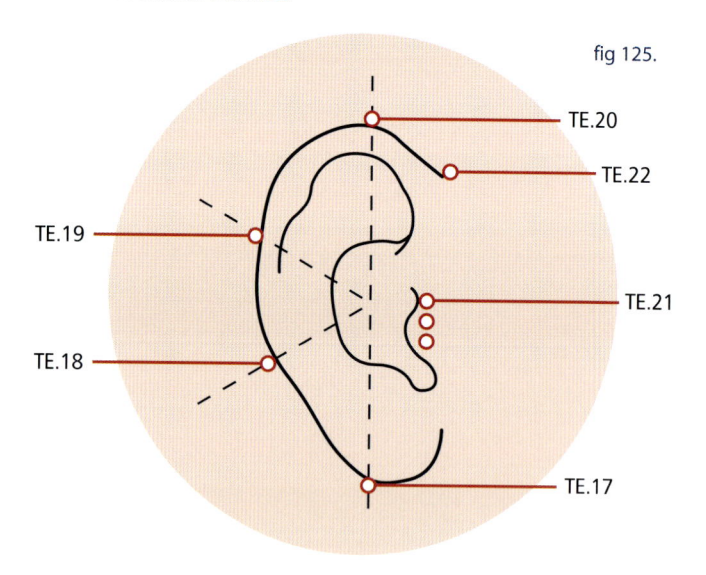

ACUPUNCTURE POINTS

TRIPLE ENERGISER 23

Location: In the depression at the lateral end of the eyebrow, at the bony margin of the orbit (fig 126).

Needling: Perpendicular 0.2 cun or transverse 0.5 cun.

Note: The superficial temporal artery lies close to this point.

Uses: (i) One sided headache. (ii) Twitching of the eyelid (blepharospasm).

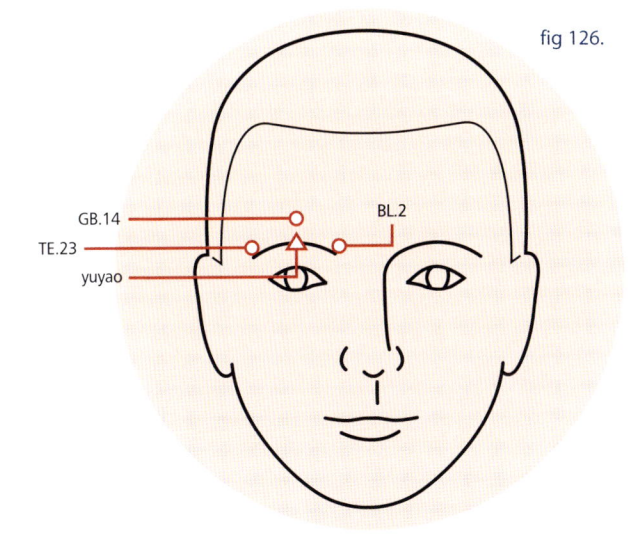

fig 126.

ACUPUNCTURE POINTS

GALL BLADDER (GB)

GALL BLADDER 1

Location: In the hollow on the lateral side of the orbit, approximately 0.5 cun lateral to the outer canthus (fig 127).

Needling: Transverse insertion posteriorly 0.2 to 0.3 cun.

Uses: (i) Diseases of the eye. (ii) *meeting point* of Gall Bladder, Small intestine and Triple energiser channels

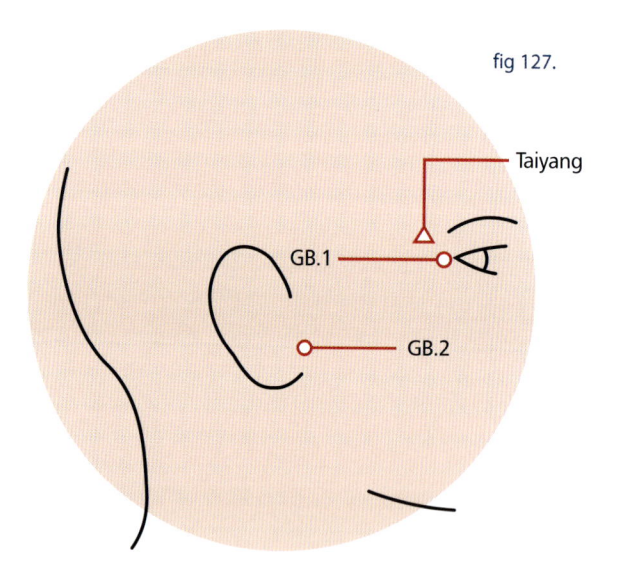

fig 127.

ACUPUNCTURE POINTS

GALL BLADDER 2

Location: In front of the ear, within the hollow between the intertragic notch and the condyloid process of the mandible (fig 128)

Needling: Perpendicular 0.5 to 1 cun.

Note: Locate the point with the mouth wide open, and relax the mouth when the needle is in position.

Uses: Diseases of the ear.

fig 128.

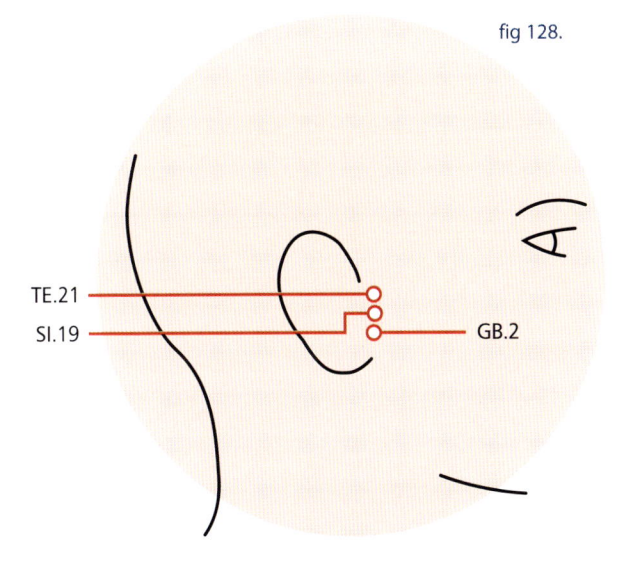

ACUPUNCTURE POINTS

GALL BLADDER 3

Location: Directly above ST-7 in a small hollow on the upper border of the zygomatic arch (fig 129)

Needling: Perpendicular insertion 0.3-0.5 cun

Note: this point lies approximately 1 cun anterior to the root of the ear.

Uses: Local point to treat ear pain

fig 129.

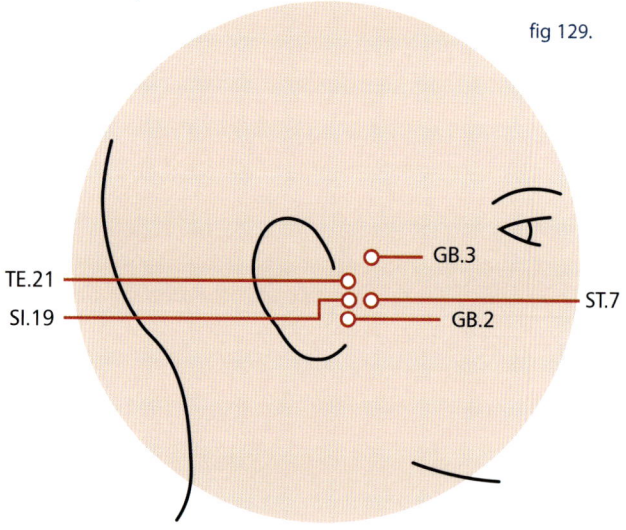

ACUPUNCTURE POINTS

GALL BLADDER 4-7

Location: Each point lies on a line joining ST-8 and GB-7 (fig 130).
- GB-4 lies ¼ of the distance from ST-8,
- GB-5 lies ½ of the distance from ST-8
- GB-6 lies ¾ of the distance from ST-8
- GB-7 is located at the junction of a horizontal line drawn from the apex of the ear and a vertical line drawn from the anterior border of the ear (fig 131).

Needling: Transverse insertion 0.3-1.0 cun

Uses: (i) One sided headache (ii) Jaw and temporomandibular joint (TMJ) pain

GALL BLADDER 8

Location: 1 cun directly above the apex of the ear (fig 131)

Needling: Transverse insertion 0.3-1.0 cun

Note: TE-20 lies at the ear apex (see page 125)

Uses: Local point for one sided headache

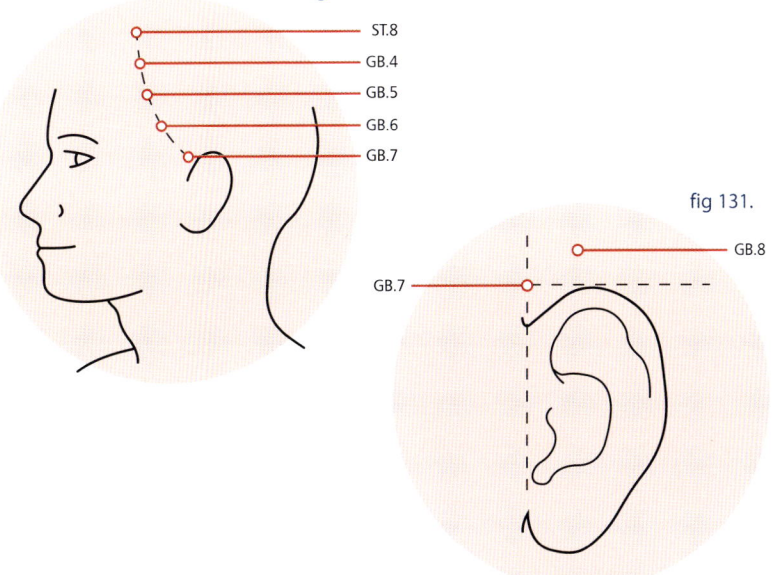

fig 130.

ST.8
GB.4
GB.5
GB.6
GB.7

fig 131.

GB.8
GB.7

ACUPUNCTURE POINTS

GALL BLADDER 9 / 10 / 11

Location: Each point lies on a line curving posterior to the ear (fig 132).
- GB-9 lies 0.5 cun posterior to GB-8.
- GB-10 lies at the upper 1/3rd
- GB-11 at the lower 1/3rd of the curved line connecting GB-9 to GB-12.

Needling: Transverse insertion 0.3-1.0 cun

Uses: (i) one sided headache (ii) pain behind the ear

fig 132.

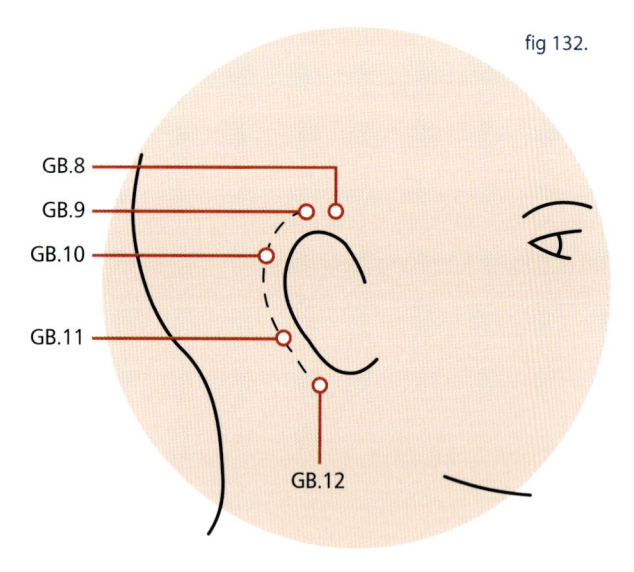

ACUPUNCTURE POINTS

GALL BLADDER 12

Location: In the depression slightly posterior and inferior to the mastoid process (fig 133).

Needling: 0.3 - 0.5 cun oblique.

Uses: (i) One sided headache referring pain behind the ear. (ii) traditionally used to eliminate *pathogenic wind*.

fig 133.

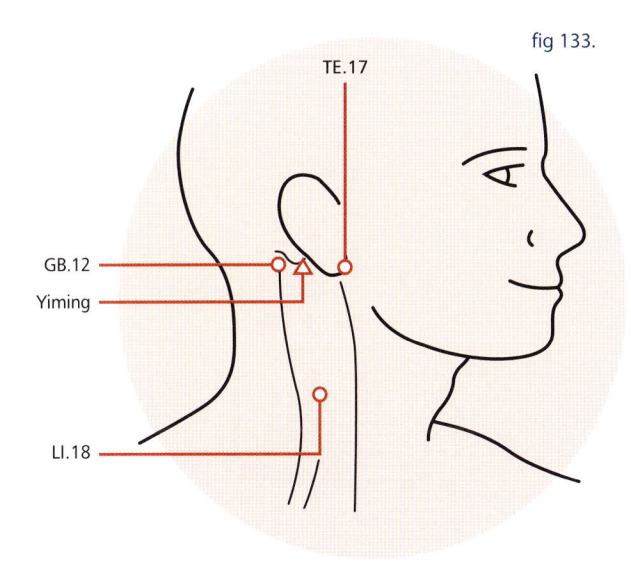

ACUPUNCTURE POINTS

GALL BLADDER 13

Location: On the forehead 3 cun lateral to the midline and 0.5 cun superior to the anterior hairline (fig 134)

Needling: Transverse insertion 0.5-0.8 cun

Uses: (i) frontal headache (ii) said to benefit the eyes.

fig 134.

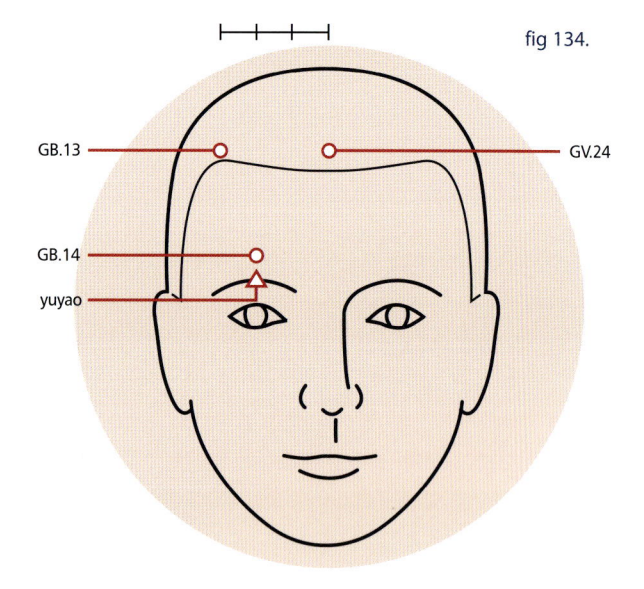

GB.13
GV.24
GB.14
yuyao

ACUPUNCTURE POINTS

GALL BLADDER 14

Location: On the forehead directly above the pupil, 1 cun superior to the middle of the eyebrow (fig 135).

Needling: 0.3 – 0.5 cun transverse

Uses: (i) Frontal headache. (ii) Drooping eye lid.

fig 135.

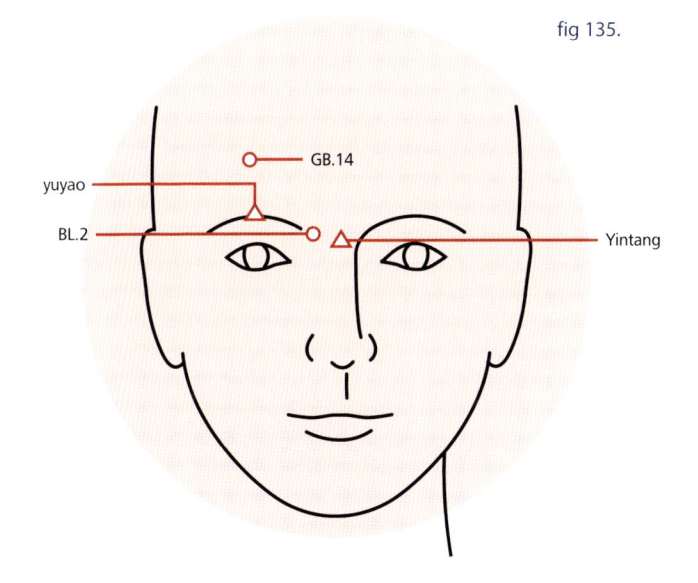

ACUPUNCTURE POINTS

GALL BLADDER 15 – 19

Location: Each point lies on a line from GB-14 over the head to GB-20 (fig 136).
- GB-15 lies 0.5 cun above the anterior hairline
- GB-16 lies 1.5 cun above the anterior hairline
- GB-17 lies 2.5 cun above the anterior hairline
- GB-18 lies 4 cun above the anterior hairline
- GB-19 lies 1.5 cun above GB-20.

Needling: Transverse insertion 0.3-1.0 cun

Note: The Gall Bladder meridian runs on the pupil line 2.25 cun lateral to the midline.

Uses: (i) Headache (ii) traditionally used to eliminate *wind pathogen*.

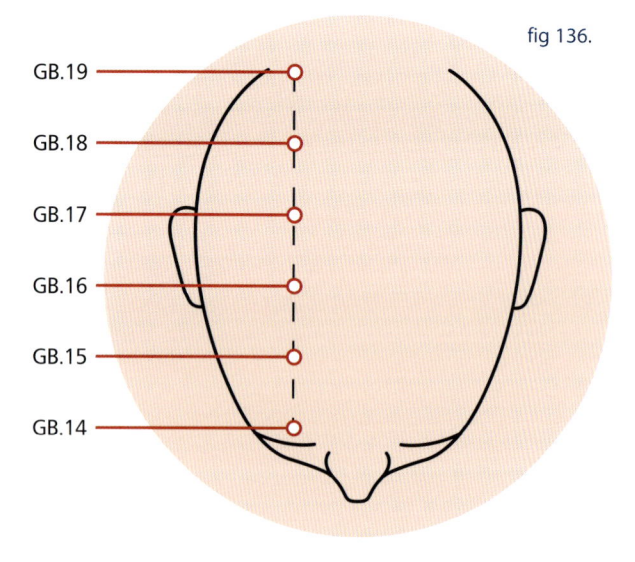

fig 136.

ACUPUNCTURE POINTS

GALL BLADDER 20

Location: Below the occiput, approximately midway between the mastoid process (GB-12) and the external occipital protuberance (GV-16) (fig 137).

Needling: Oblique insertion directed towards the tip of the nose, 0.8 – 1.2 cun.

Note: (i) The vertebral artery lies medial to this point. (ii) The point lies between the origins of the sternomastoid and trapezius muscles.

Uses: (i) Major point in the treatment of all forms of headache. (ii) Local point for neck pain. (iii) *meeting point* of the Gall Bladder and Triple Energiser channels with the Yang Motility and Yang Linking vessels.

fig 137.

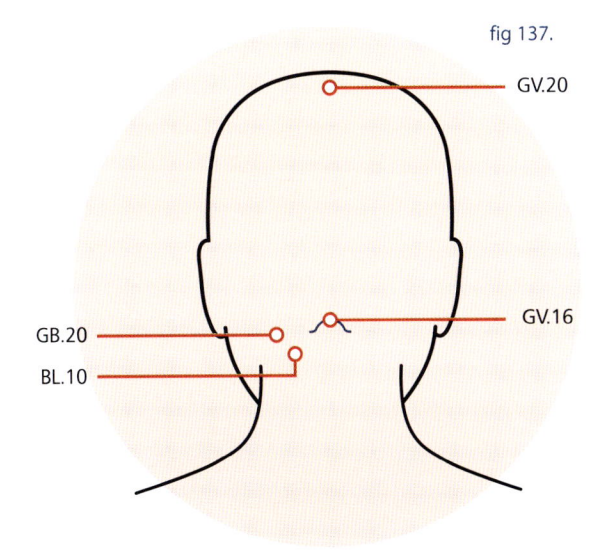

ACUPUNCTURE POINTS

GALL BLADDER 21

Location: At the level of the midpoint between C7 (GV-14) and the tip of the acromion, at the highest point of the trapezius muscle (fig 138).

Needling: 0.5 – 0.8 cun oblique anteriorly or posteriorly.

Note: (i) The trapezius muscle may be gripped and lifted to aid needling in thin subjects. (ii) TE-15 lies inferior and slightly medial to this point.

Uses: (i) Pain and stiffness in the neck and shoulder. (ii) *meeting point* of the GB, TE, ST channels with the Yang Linking vessel

fig 138.

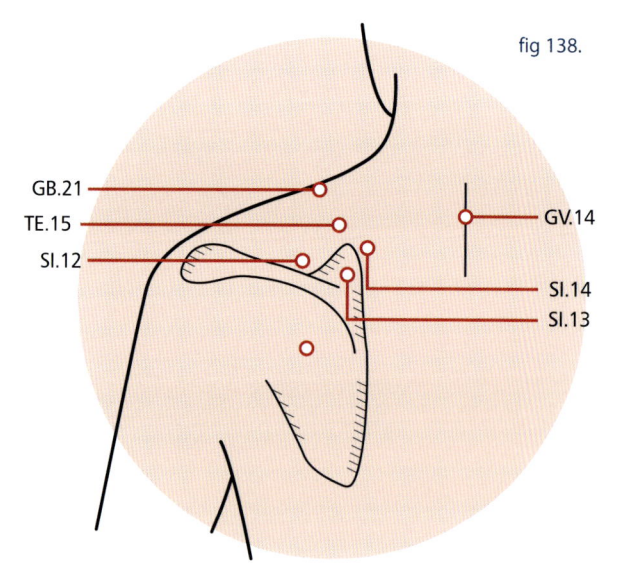

ACUPUNCTURE POINTS

GALL BLADDER 22 - 28

Location: Each point lies on the antero-lateral aspect of the chest within the relevant intercostal space (ICS) (fig 139).

- GB-22 lies on the mid axillary line in the 5th ICS
- GB-23 lies in the 5th ICS, 1.0 cun anterior to GB-22
- GB-24 lies in the 7th ICS on the nipple (mamillary) line
- GB-25 lies anterior and inferior to the free end of the 12th rib
- GB-26 lies anterior and inferior to the free end of the 11th rib, level with the umbilicus and below LR-13
- GB-27 lies anterior to the anterior superior iliac spine (ASIS).
- GB-28 lies 0.5 cun anterior and interior to GB-27

Needling: Points GB-22 to GB-26 are needled using an oblique insertion 0.5 cun. GB-27 and GB-28 may be needled using a perpendicular or oblique insertion 1.0 to 1.5 cun.

Uses: (i) used to treat pain in the costal region (ii) traditionally used for epigastric pain and *rebellious qi*, (iii) GB-24 is the *front Mu point* of the Gallbladder, GB-25 the *front Mu point* of the Kidney.

fig 139.

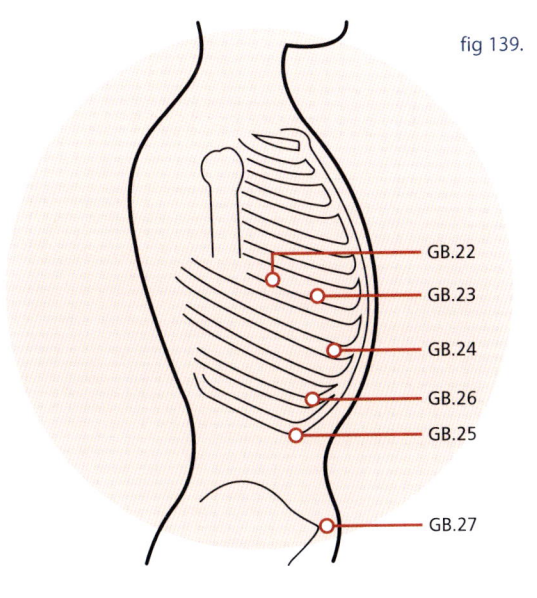

ACUPUNCTURE POINTS

GALL BLADDER 29

Location: On the lateral aspect of the hip joint, between the anterior superior iliac spine (ASIS) and apex of the greater trochanter (fig 140).

Needling: Perpendicular insertion 1- 1.5 cun.

Uses: Local point for hip pain.

fig 140.

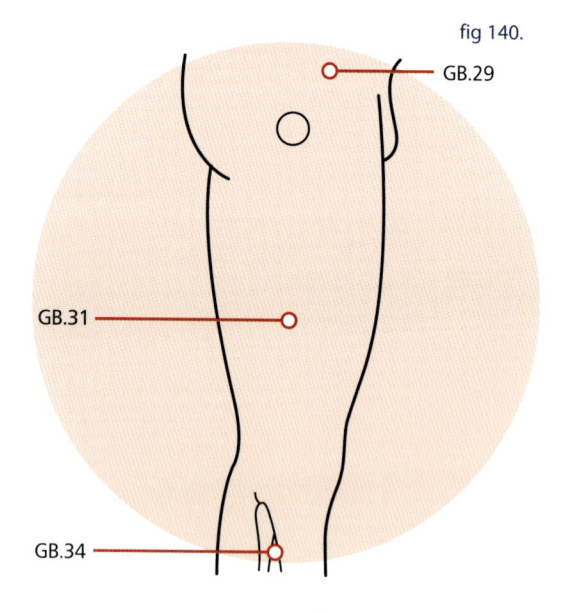

ACUPUNCTURE POINTS

GALL BLADDER 30

Location: On the postero-lateral aspect of the hip joint, one third of the distance between the apex of the greater trochanter and the sacral hiatus (GV-2) (fig 141).

Needling: Perpendicular insertion 2 to 3 cun.

Uses: Much used point for lumbo-sacral pain and hip pain.

fig 141.

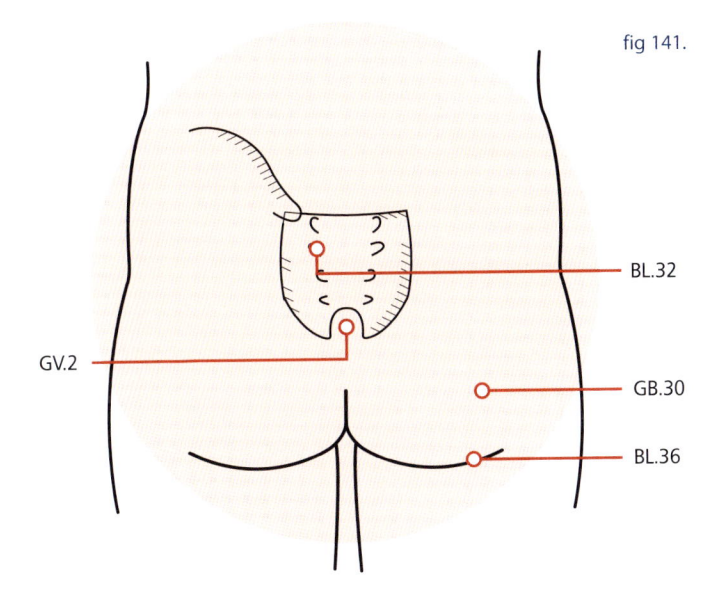

- BL.32
- GV.2
- GB.30
- BL.36

ACUPUNCTURE POINTS

GALL BLADDER 31 - 32

Location: On the lateral aspect of the thigh, directly below the greater trochanter.
- GB-31 lies 7 cun superior to the popliteal crease
- GB-32 lies 5 cun superior to the popliteal crease (fig 142).

Needling: Perpendicular or oblique insertion 1 to 2 cun.

Note: (i) With the subject standing and the arm hanging relaxed at the side of the body, GB-31 lies approximately at the tip of the middle finger. (ii) On a line between the highest point of the Greater Trochanter and the knee joint, GB-32 lies just proximal to the lower ¼.

Uses: Lateral leg pain. Often used following hemiplegia.

GALL BLADDER 33

Location: Above the lateral aspect of the knee, the point lies between the lateral epicondyle and the tendon of Biceps Femoris (fig 142)

Needling: Perpendicular insertion 1.0-2.0 cun

Uses: Lateral knee pain

fig 142.

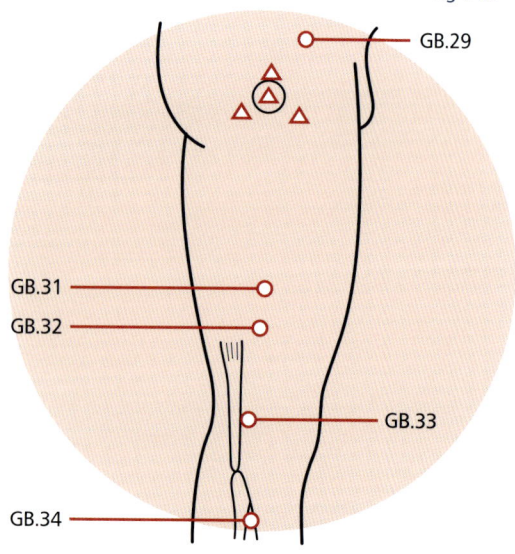

ACUPUNCTURE POINTS

GALL BLADDER 34

Location: Below the lateral aspect of the knee, 1 cun anterior and inferior to the head of the fibula (fig 143).

Needling: Perpendicular or oblique insertion 1 to 1.5 cun.

Note: The deep peroneal nerve lies close to this point, and the superficial peroneal nerve lies above.

Uses: (i) Major point for joint pain in general, GB-34 is the *influential point* for muscle and tendon. (ii) *Heavenly star* point for cold bi syndrome.

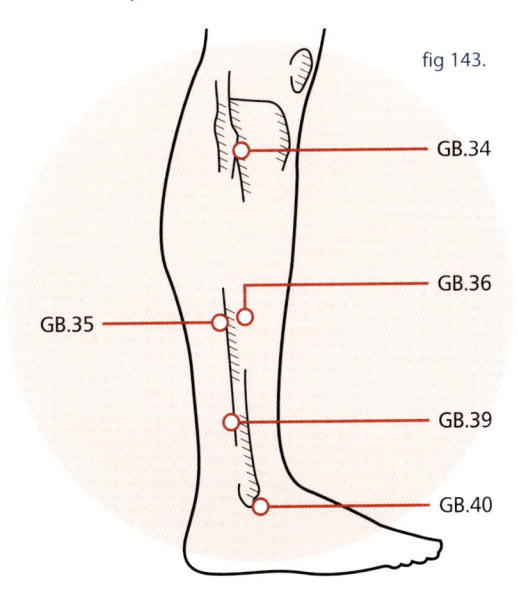

fig 143.

ACUPUNCTURE POINTS

GALL BLADDER 35 / 36

Location: Each point is located 7 cun superior to the apex of the lateral malleolus (fig 144).
- GB-35 lies posterior to the fibular
- GB-36 lies anterior to the fibula.

Needling: Perpendicular insertion 0.5-1.5 cun

Note: These points also lie at the midpoint of a line joining GB-34 and the apex of the lateral malleolus

Uses: (i) Lateral shin pain (ii) GB-35 is the *Xi-cleft* point of the Yang Linking vessel, GB-36 the *Xi-cleft* point of the Gall Bladder channel.

GALL BLADDER 37

Location: On the lateral aspect of the shin, 5.0 cun superior to the apex of the lateral malleolus. The point lies anterior to the fibular border (fig 144).

Needling: Perpendicular insertion 1.0 to 1.5 cun

Uses: (i) local shin pain and 'shin splints' (ii) *Luo connecting point* of the Gallbladder channel (iii) traditionally said to *benefit the eyes*.

GALL BLADDER 38

Location: Above the ankle joint 4 cun superior to the apex of the lateral malleolus, and anterior to the fibula. (fig 144)

Needling: Perpendicular insertion 0.5- 1.0 cun.

Uses: (i) Local point for lower lateral leg pain.

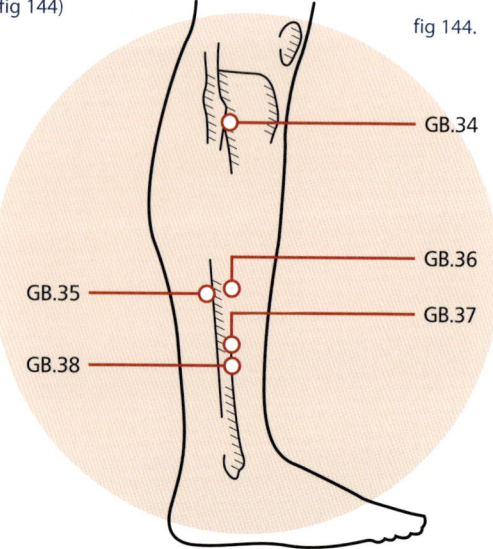

fig 144.

ACUPUNCTURE POINTS

GALL BLADDER 39

Location: Above the ankle joint 3 cun superior to the apex of the lateral malleolus, and posterior to the fibula. (fig 145).

Note: The point lies between the fibula and peroneal tendons.

Needling: Perpendicular insertion 1 to 1.5 cun.

Uses: (i) Local point for lower lateral leg pain. (ii) *Influential point* for bone marrow (iii) *Heavenly star* point for *fixed bi* syndrome.

GALL BLADDER 40

Location: At the ankle joint in the depression anterior and inferior to the lateral malleolus. (fig 145)

Needling: Perpendicular insertion 0.5 – 0.8 cun.

Note: The point lies lateral to the tendon of extensor digitorum longus. GB-40 is the lateral 'eye' of the ankle joint, the medial being SP-5.

Uses: (i) Ankle joint pain. (ii) *Source* point of the Gall Bladder channel.

fig 145.

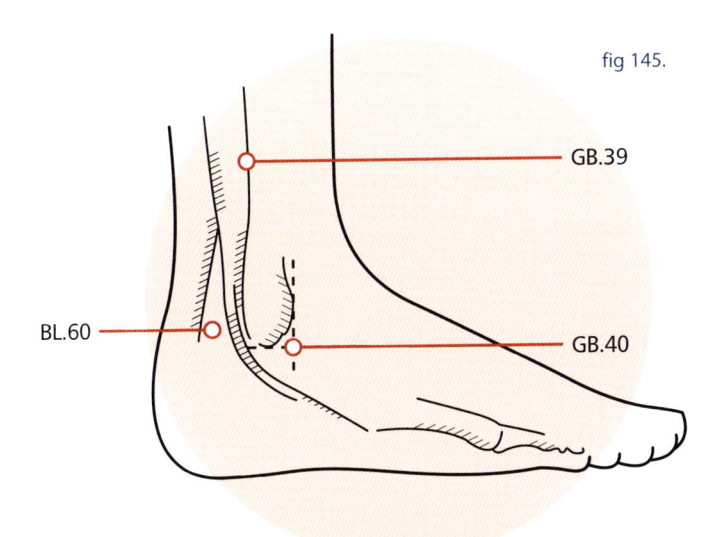

ACUPUNCTURE POINTS

GALL BLADDER 41

Location: In the depression distal to the junction of the 4th and 5th metatarsal bones (fig. 146).

Needling: 0.5 cun perpendicular

Note: The point lies on the lateral side of extensor digitorum longus. The needle should pass between the metatarsal shafts and not touch the bone.

Uses: (i) Traditionally used for temporal headache and eye pain. (ii) *Confluence point* of the Girdling vessel

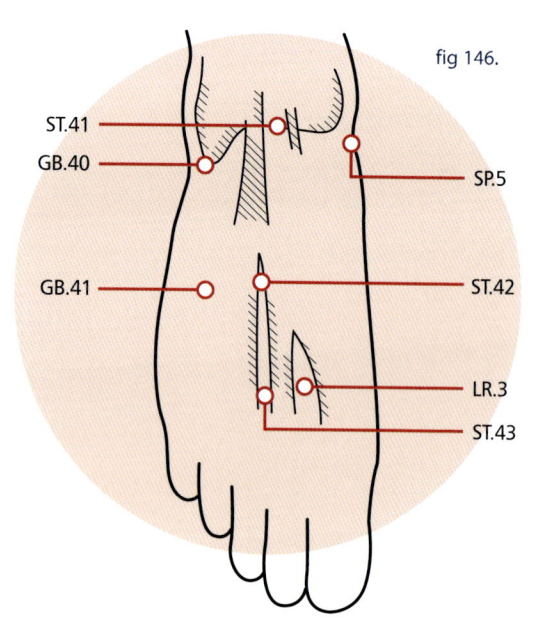

fig 146.

ACUPUNCTURE POINTS

GALL BLADDER 42
Location: Between the 4th and 5th metatarsals, proximal to the MCP joints. The point lies medial to the tendon of extensor digitorum longus (fig 147)

Needling: Perpendicular insertion 0.5-0.8 cun

Uses: (i) Local point for interdigital pain (ii) Traditionally said to *move Liver qi* and *clear heat* in the Gall Bladder especially in cases of headache.

GALL BLADDER 43
Location: In the web space between the 4th and 5th toes (fig 147).

Needling: Perpendicular 0.3 cun

Notes: This point is also one of the *Bafeng* extra points.

Uses: (i) Traditionally used to treat headaches and tinnitus. (ii) As a *Bafeng* point it may be used for toe disorders.

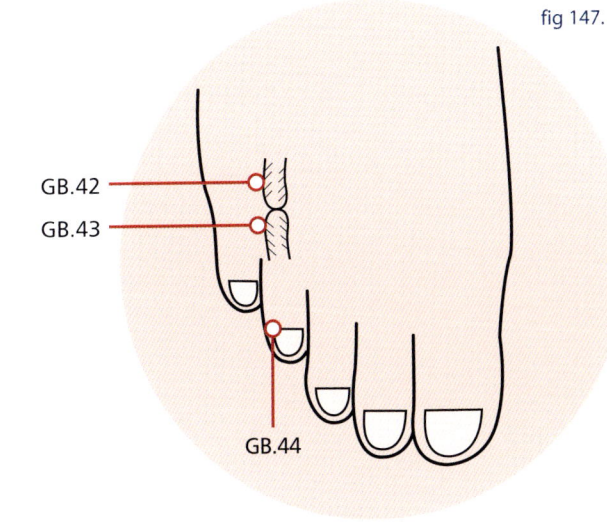

fig 147.

ACUPUNCTURE POINTS

GALL BLADDER 44

Location: Lateral nail point of the 4th toe (fig 148).

Needling: 0.1 cun perpendicular

Uses: Traditionally used to treat acute ear diseases.

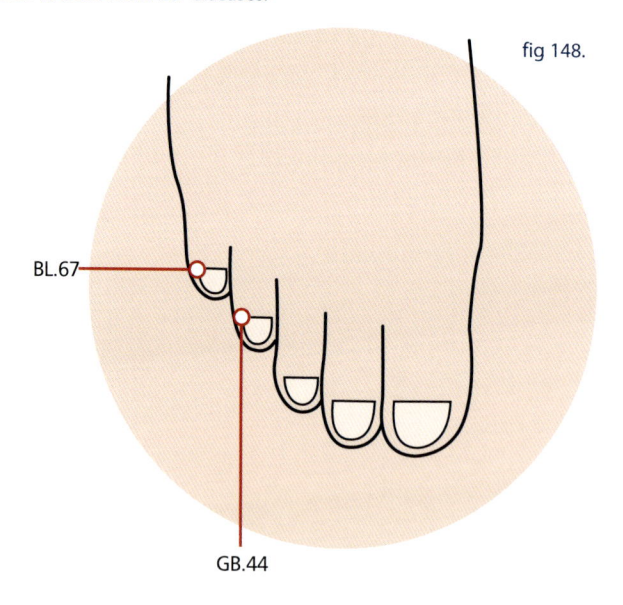

fig 148.

BL.67

GB.44

ACUPUNCTURE POINTS

LIVER (LV)

LIVER 1

Location: On the lateral nail point of the 1st (big) toe (fig 149).

Needling: Perpendicular insertion directed proximally 0.1 cun.

Uses: Traditionally used for hernias.

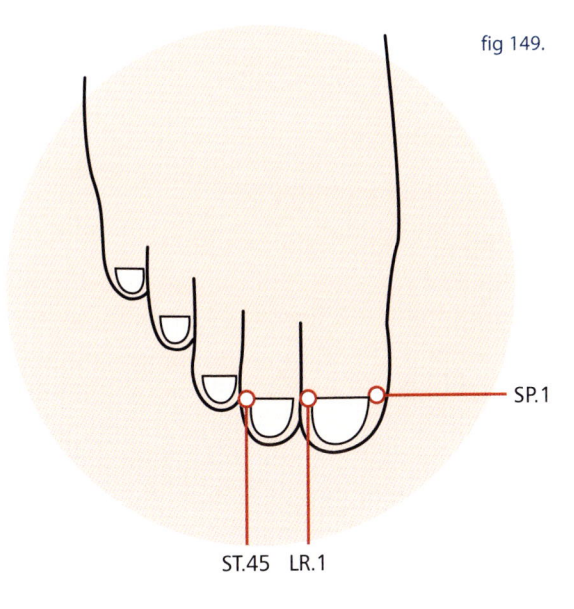

fig 149.

SP.1

ST.45   LR.1

ACUPUNCTURE POINTS

LIVER 2

Location: On the dorsum of the foot, in the web space between the first and second toes (fig 150).

Needling: Perpendicular 0.5 cun.

Note: This is one of a group of extra points called the *'Bafeng'*.

Uses: (i) Traditionally used to treat headaches and dizziness. (ii) May also be used to regulate menstruation. (iii) As one of the *Bafeng* points, used to treat disorders of the toes.

LIVER 3

Location: On the dorsum of the foot, in the depression distal to the junction of the first and second metatarsal bones (fig 150).

Needling: Perpendicular 0.5 – 0.8 cun

Note: To find the point, run the finger along the interspace between the two toes until it rests in the depression at the junction of the 1st and 2nd metatarsals.

Uses: (i) With point LI-4 this is one of the 'four gates' (four bars) points used to relieve pain and generally harmonise the body. (ii) *Source point* of the Liver channel. (iii) *Heavenly star* point for stress and anxiety.

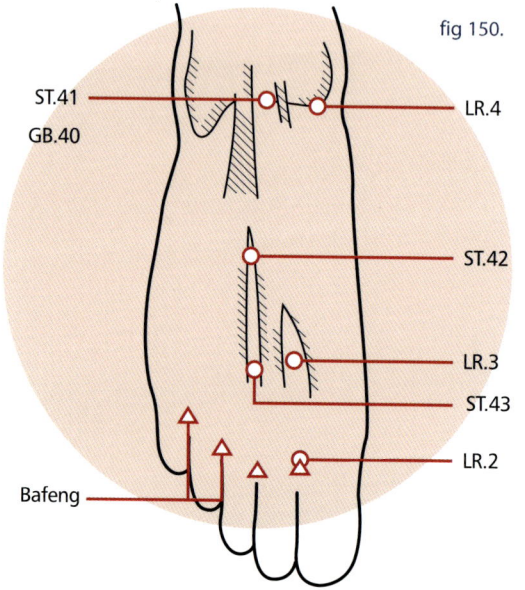

fig 150.

ST.41
GB.40
LR.4
ST.42
LR.3
ST.43
LR.2
Bafeng

ACUPUNCTURE POINTS

LIVER 4

Location: On the inside of the ankle 1 cun anterior to the apex of the medial malleolus. (fig 151)

Needling: Perpendicular or oblique insertion 0.3-0.5 cun

Uses: Medial ankle pain

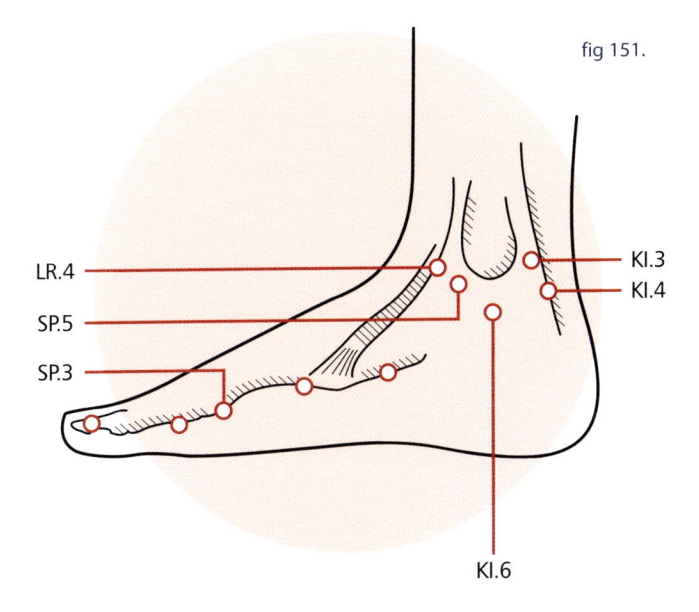

fig 151.

ACUPUNCTURE POINTS

LIVER 5/6

Location: On the medial aspect of the shin (fig 152)
LR-5 lies 5 cun above the apex of the medial malleolus, between the tibia and the gastrocnemius muscle,
LR-6 lies 7 cun above the apex of the malleolus between the tibia and the gastrocnemius muscle

Needling: Oblique insertion 0.5 to 0.8 cun.

Note: (i) As the distance between the apex of the medial malleolus and the knee joint line is 15 cun, LR-5 lies at the junction of the lower 1/3rd of that line. (ii) LR-6 lies the width of 2 hands (6 cun) and 1 thumb (1 cun) above the malleolar apex.

Uses: (i) LR-5 is traditionally used for gynaecological disorders and inflammation of the male genitalia. (ii) LR-5 is the *Luo-connecting* point of the Liver channel, LR-6 the *Xi-cleft* point of the Liver channel.

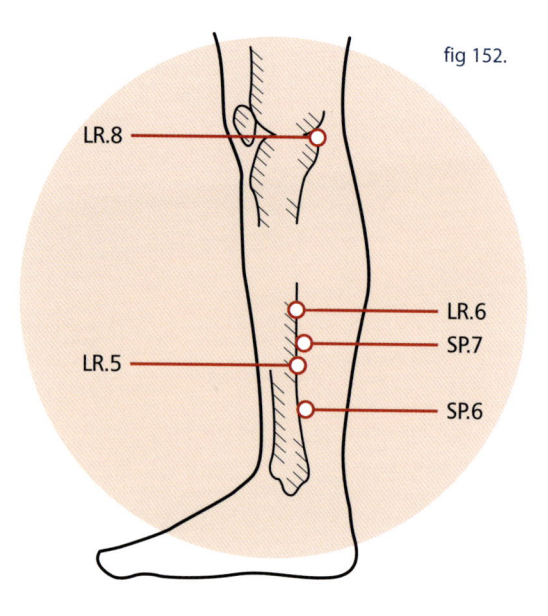

fig 152.

ACUPUNCTURE POINTS

LIVER 7

Location: On the inner aspect of the knee 1 cun posterior to SP-9 (fig 153)

Needling: Perpendicular insertion 1.0-2.0 cun

Uses: Local point for medial knee pain

LIVER 8

Location: Just superior to the medial end of the popliteal crease, in the depression anterior to the tendons of semitendinosus and semimembranosus (fig 53)

Needling: Perpendicular insertion 1 to 1.5 cun

Note: This point lies approximately 1 cun anterior to KI-10.

Uses: (i) Local point for medial knee pain and tendonitis of the medial hamstrings. (ii) Traditionally used to treat prolapse of the uterus and pain in the genitals.

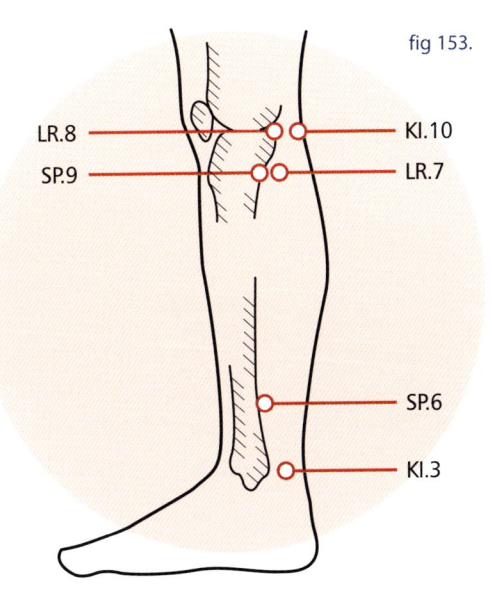

fig 153.

ACUPUNCTURE POINTS

LIVER 9

Location: Superior to the medial aspect of the knee joint, 4 cun above LR-8 (fig 154).

Needling: Perpendicular insertion 1.0-2.0 cun

Note: LR-9 lies medial to the Sartorius muscle

Uses: (i) Medial / Superior knee pain

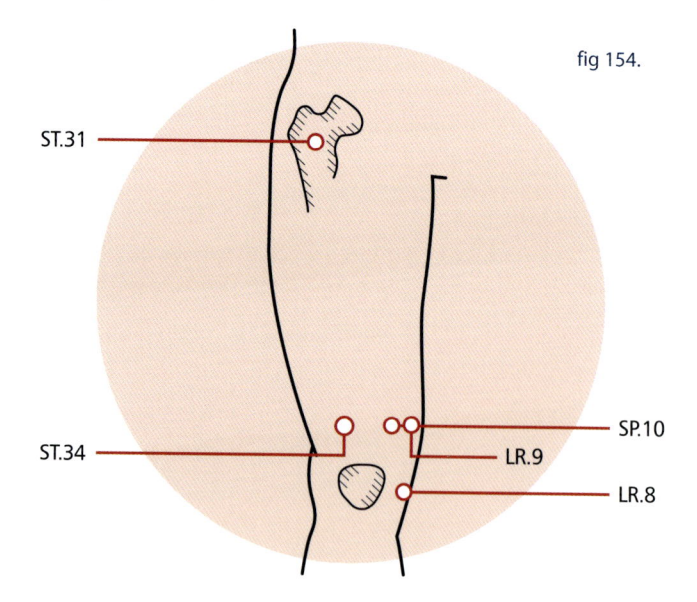

fig 154.

ACUPUNCTURE POINTS

LIVER 10 / 11

Location: On the antero-medial aspect of the thigh, on the lateral aspect of Adductor Longus (fig 155).
LR-10 lies 3 cun inferior to the upper border of the symphysis pubis
LR-11 lies 2 cun inferior to the upper border of the symphysis pubis

Needling: Perpendicular insertion 0.5-1.5 cun

Note: These point may also be found relative to ST-30 (2 cun lateral to the upper border of the symphysis). LR-11 lies 2 cun inferior and LR-10 3 cun inferior to ST-30.

Uses: Local points for pain in the adductor muscles.

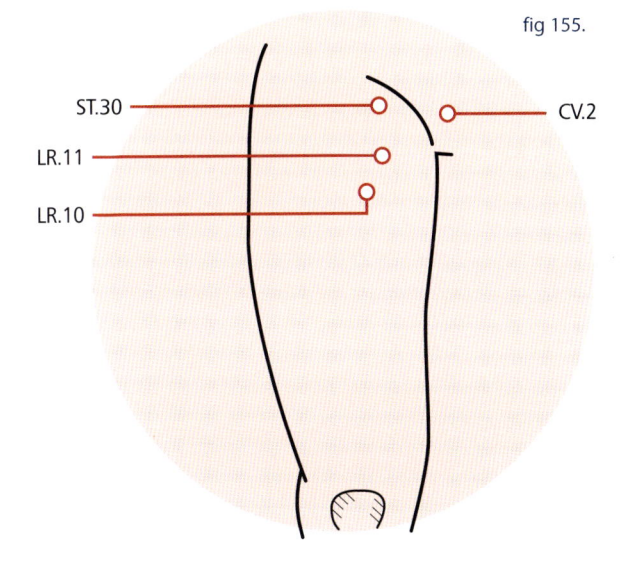

fig 155.

ACUPUNCTURE POINTS

LIVER 12

Location: On the inguinal crease, 2.5 cun lateral to the midline and 1 cun below the superior border of the symphysis pubis (fig 156).

Needling: Oblique insertion angled medially 0.5 cun

Uses: (i) local point for groin pain (ii) traditionally used to treat pain in the genitals

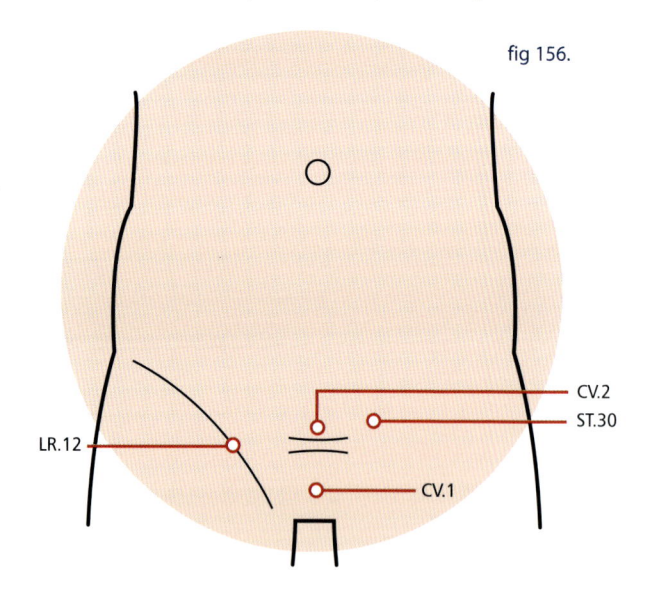

fig 156.

ACUPUNCTURE POINTS

LIVER 13

Location: Just inferior to the free end of the 11th rib (fig 157).

Needling: 0.8 cun transverse.

Note: This point lies approximately on the mid-axillary line, 1 cun superior to the umbilicus

Uses: (i) Local point for lateral costal pain. (ii) *Front-Mu* point of the Spleen (iii) Influential point of the Zang organs

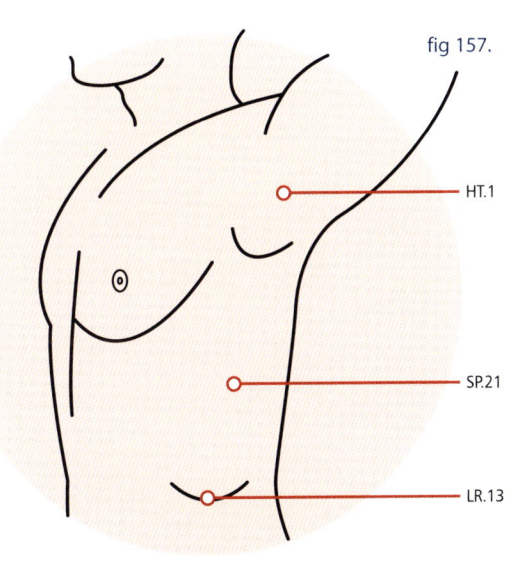

fig 157.

HT.1

SP.21

LR.13

ACUPUNCTURE POINTS

LIVER 14

Location: On the mamillary (nipple) line in the sixth intercostals space 4 cun lateral to the midline (fig 158).

Needling: Oblique subcutaneous insertion 0.5 to 0.8 cun

Uses: *Front Mu* (collecting) point of the Liver. Traditionally used for hypo chondric pain.

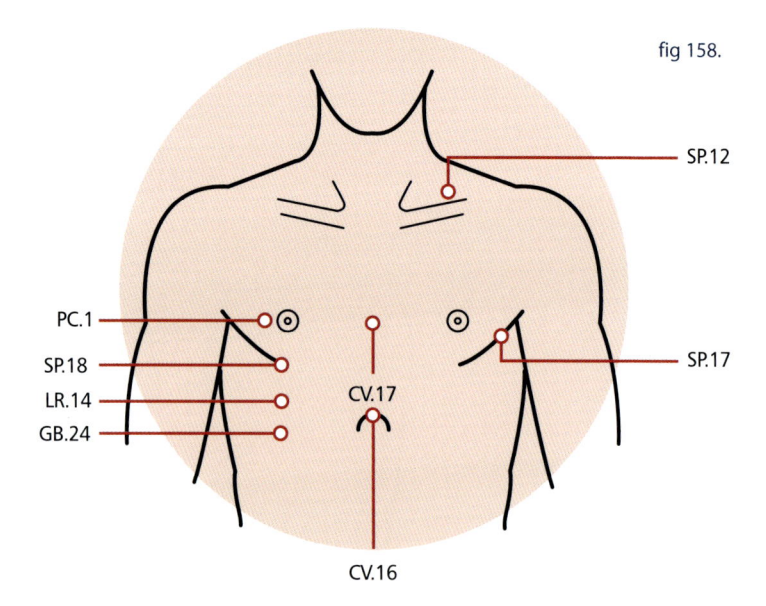

fig 158.

ACUPUNCTURE POINTS

GOVERNING VESSEL (GV)

GOVERNING VESSEL 1
Location: On the midline midway between the tip of the coccyx and the anus (fig 159)

Needling: Perpendicular insertion 0.5 to 1 cun.

Note: Needle either with the patient side lying with the upper leg drawn up, or in prone.

Uses: Traditionally used to treat haemorrhoids.

GOVERNING VESSEL 2
Location: Within the sacral hiatus (fig 159).

Needling: Oblique insertion directed cranially 0.5 – 1.0 cun

Uses: Local point for Coccygea, (Coccydynia).

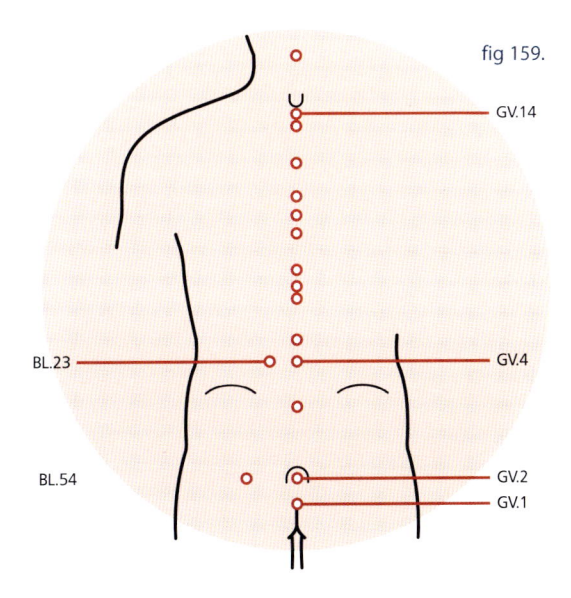

fig 159.

- GV.14
- GV.4
- BL.23
- BL.54
- GV.2
- GV.1

ACUPUNCTURE POINTS

GOVERNING VESSEL 3 - 13

Location: Each point lies in the midline of the lumbar and thoracic spine in the depression below the spinous processes (fig 160).

Needling: Oblique insertion 0.5 to 1 cun, directed cranially

Note: (i) The depth of the spinal canal is between 1.0 to 2.0cms below the surface depending on body size. A needle less that 1cms long should be used and angled obliquely.

Uses: (i) Used for local central spinal pain (ii) traditionally used to treat fever (febrile diseases) by *draining heat* (iii) calm the mind / spirit (*Shen*) (iv) effect the internal organs

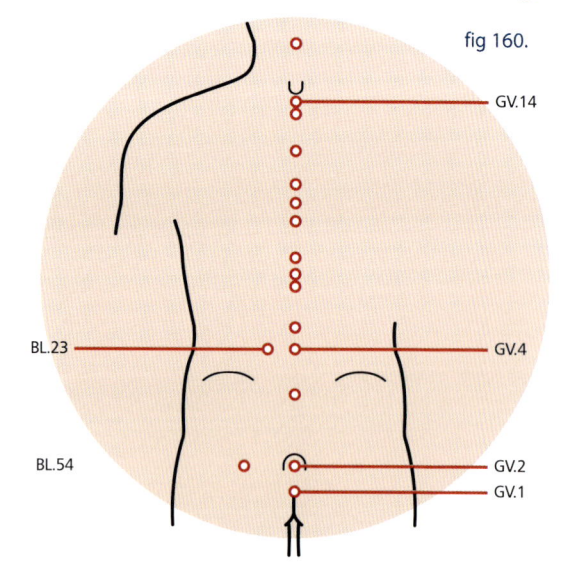

fig 160.

Point	Level	Use (in addition to local pain)	Point	Level	Use (in addition to local pain)
GV-3	L3	Impotence	GV-9	T7	Strengthens Spleen & drains *damp*
GV-4	L4	Tonifies *Yang*	GV-10	T6	Tonifies *Yang*
GV-5	L1	Tonifies lower part of TE	GV-11	T5	Tonifies HT & LU, *calms the spirit*
GV-6	T11	Tonifies Spleen & drains *damp*	GV-12	T3	Dispels wind pathogen from LU & treats cough
GV-7	T10	Tonifies middle part of TE	GV-13	T1	Dispels pathogens, used in Malaria
GV-8	T9	Calms Liver & treats Jaundice			

ACUPUNCTURE POINTS

GOVERNING VESSEL 14

Location: At the base of the neck in the depression below the spinous process of C7 (fig 161).
Needling: Oblique cranial insertion 0.5 to 1 cun.

Uses: (i) Meeting point of all six yang channels. (ii) Traditionally used to reduce fever and night sweats. (iii) Local point for neck pain.

fig 161.

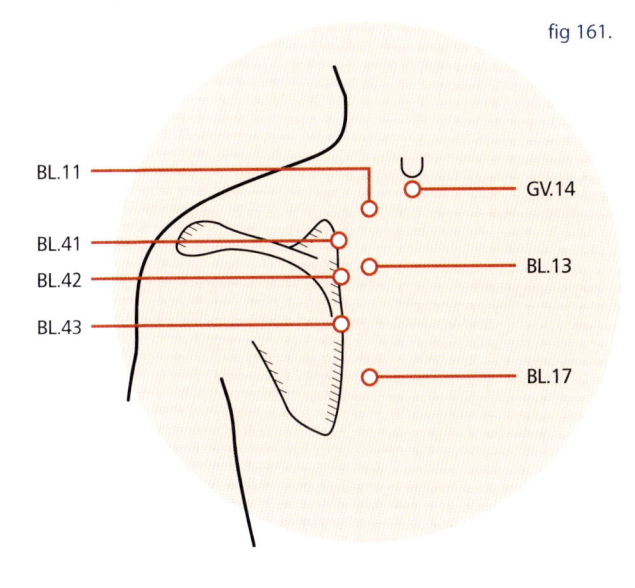

ACUPUNCTURE POINTS

GOVERNING VESSEL 15
Location: At the nape of the neck, in the depression 0.5 cun inferior to GV-16 (fig 162).

Needling: Perpendicular insertion slightly inferiorly 0.5 to 1 cun.

Uses: Traditionally used for epilepsy and cerebro-vascular accident (CVA).

GOVERNING VESSEL 16
Location: At the base of the skull, in the depression directly below the external occipital protuberance. The point lies at the craniocervical junction between the upper attachments of the trapezius muscle (fig 162).

Needling: 0.5 cun perpendicular

Uses: Traditionally used for headache, local point for sub-occipital pain.

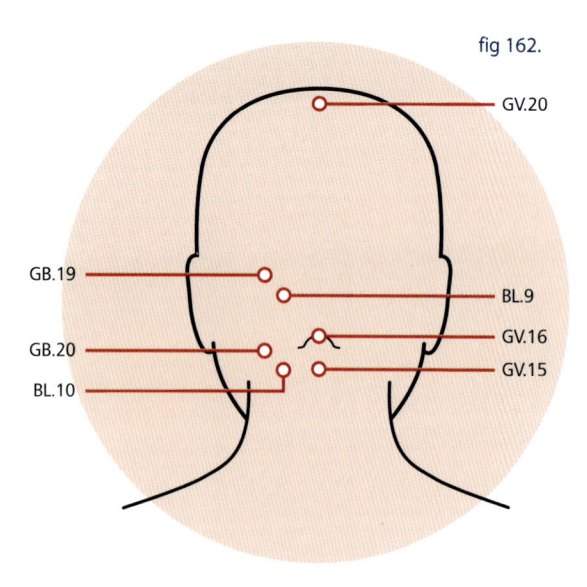

fig 162.

ACUPUNCTURE POINTS

GOVERNING VESSEL 17 / 18 / 19

Location: On the central line each point lies 1.5 cun above the previous point (fig 163).
GV-17 lies 1.5 cun above GV-16
GV-18 lies 1.5 cun above GV-17 (3.0 cun above GV-16)
GV-19 lies 1.5 cun above GV-18 (4.5 cun above GV-16)

Needling: Transverse insertion 0.5-1.0 cun

Uses: (i) Local pain relief and headache (ii) calming effect

fig 163.

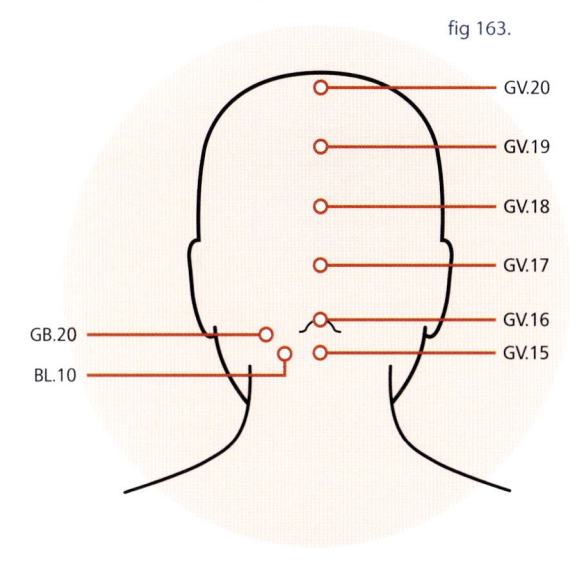

ACUPUNCTURE POINTS

GOVERNING VESSEL 20

Location: At the vertex of the head, midway between a line drawn between the two auricular apices (fig 164).

Needling: Transverse insertion 0.5 cun

Note: (i) The point may be found by placing the heels of the hands on the glabella anteriorly and the external occipital protuberance posteriorly. GV-20 lies 1 cun posterior to the meeting point of the middle fingers (ii) Standing behind the supine patient, the therapist places their hands on either side of the patients head with the little fingers touching the apex of the ears. GV-20 is found at the point where the thumb tips touch in a shallow depression at the vertex of the head (iii) This point should not be needled in infants

Uses: (i) Traditionally for vertigo and headache. (ii) Pacifies *wind pathogen*.

fig 164.

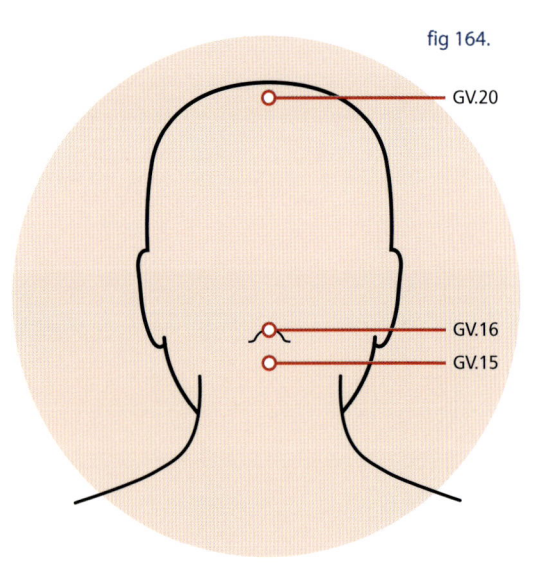

ACUPUNCTURE POINTS

GOVERNING VESSEL 21 / 22 / 23 / 24

Location: Each point lies at the top of the head on the midline measuring from GV-20 at the vertex (fig 165).
GV-21 lies 1.5 cun anterior to the vertex
GV-22 lies 3 cun anterior to the vertex
GV-23 lies 4 cun anterior to the vertex
GV-24 lies 5 cun anterior to the vertex

Needling: Transverse insertion 0.5 cun

Uses: (i) Traditionally used for headache. (ii) more anterior points benefit the nose and eyes

fig 165.

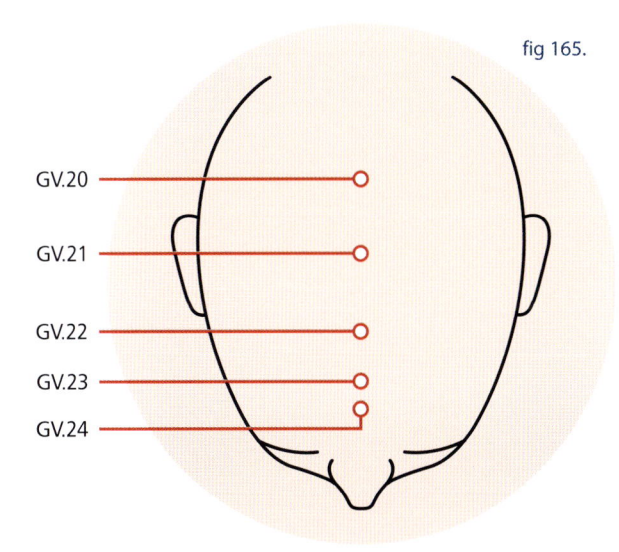

ACUPUNCTURE POINTS

GOVERNING VESSEL 25

Location: On the tip of the nose (fig 166)

Needling: Perpendicular insertion 0.2-0.3 cun

Uses: Traditionally said to benefit the nose

GOVERNING VESSEL 26

Location: On the upper lip, at the junction of the upper and middle third of the philtrum (lip groove) (fig 166).

Needling: Oblique insertion 0.3-0.5cun.

Uses: Traditionally used with sharp compression (fingernail) to restore consciousness after fainting.

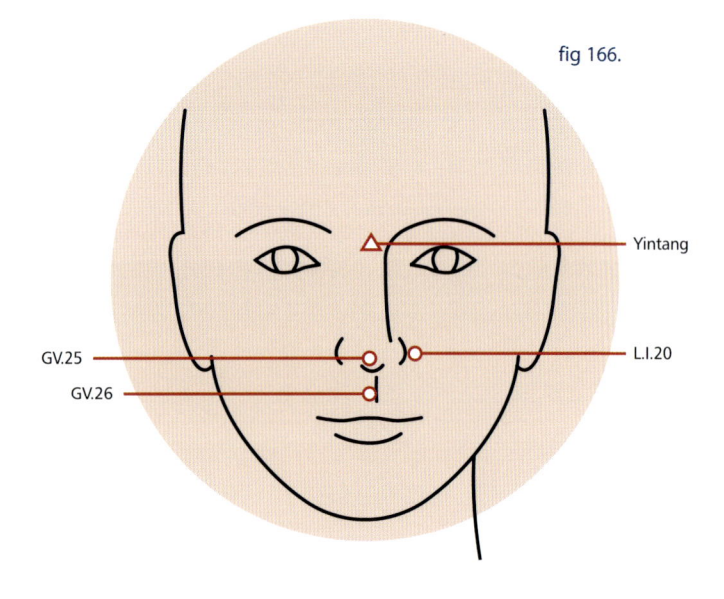

fig 166.

ACUPUNCTURE POINTS

CONCEPTION VESSEL (CV)

CONCEPTION VESSEL 1
Location : On the perineum, midway between the anus and the posterior border of the genitals (fig 167).

Needling: 0.5 cun perpendicular

Uses: (i) Usually used for location only. (i) Traditionally used to genito-urinary and anal diseases.

CONCEPTION VESSEL 2
Location : In the midline, at the upper border of the pubic symphysis (fig 167).

Needling: 0.5 cun perpendicular

Uses: (i) Local point for pubic symphysis dysfunction (PSD). (ii) Traditionally used for dysmenorrhoea and dysfunction of the urinary tract.

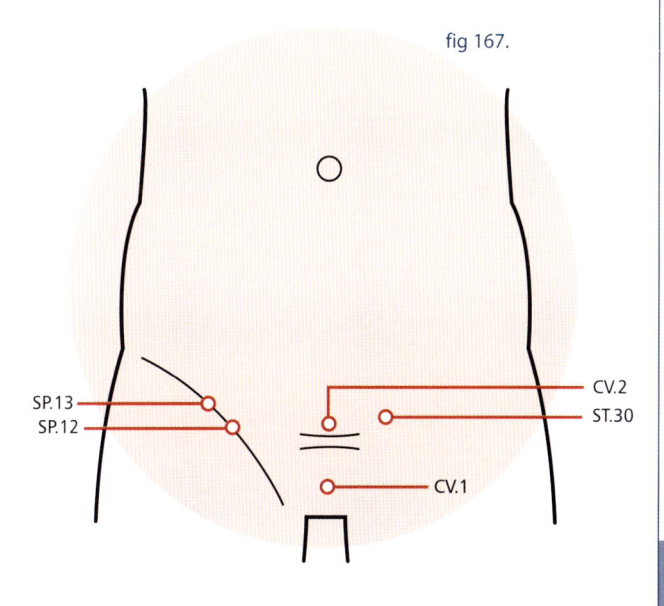

fig 167.

ACUPUNCTURE POINTS

CONCEPTION VESSEL 3 - 16

Location: Each point is measured relative to the superior border of the symphysis pubis (CV-2), the umbilicus (CV-8) or the sternocostal angle (CV-16). (fig 168 & 169)

Needling: 0.5 cun perpendicular

Uses: (i) local central pain (ii) as Front Mu points, used to affect organs beneath point location.

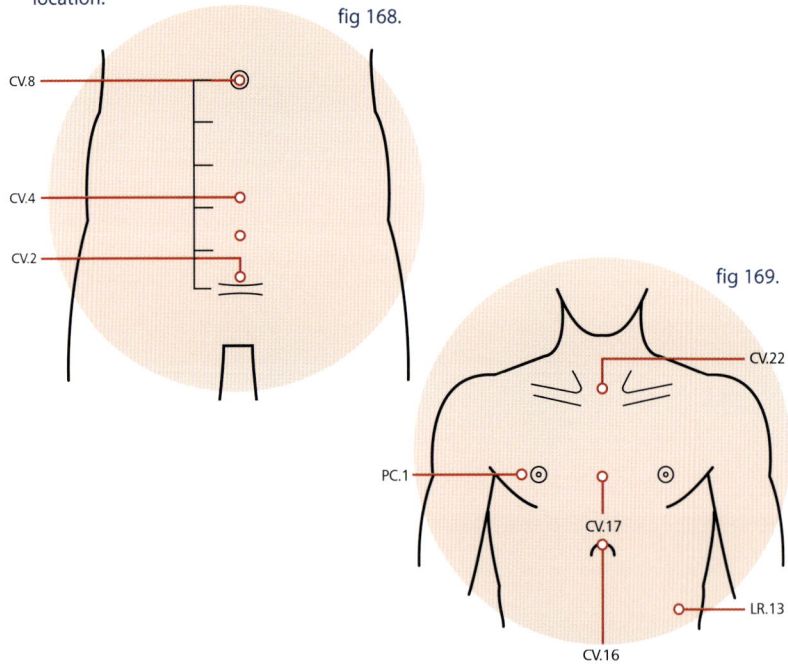

fig 168.

fig 169.

Point	Level	Use (in addition to local pain)	Point	Level	Use (in addition to local pain)
CV-2	**Superior symphysis**	Benefits urination & *invigorates KI*	CV-9	1 cun above CV-8	Treats oedema
CV-3	1 cun above CV-2	Front Mu point of BL, *drains dampness*	CV-10	2 cun above CV-8	Harmonises ST
CV-4	2 cun above CV-2	Strengthens original Qi & essence,	CV-11	3 cun above CV-8	Harmonises middle TE
		Mu point of SI	CV-12	4 cun above CV-8	*Front Mu of ST*
CV-5	3 cun above CV-2	Front Mu point of TE	CV-13	3 cun below CV-16	Harmonises ST, *descends rebellious Qi*
CV-6	4.5 cun above CV-2	Strengthens Qi	CV-14	2 cun below CV-16	*Front Mu of HT*
CV-7	1 cun below CV-8	Regulates menstruation	CV-15	11 cun below CV-16	Regulates HT, calms spirit
CV-8	**Umbilicus**	*Warms yang*, moxibustion only	CV-16	Sternocostal angle	Unbinds chest

ACUPUNCTURE POINTS

CONCEPTION VESSEL 17 / 18 / 19 / 20 / 21
Location: On the midline of the sternum, level with the intercostal spaces (fig 170).

CV-17 level with the 4th intercostal space
CV-18 level with the 3rd intercostal space
CV-19 level with the 2nd intercostal space
CV-20 level with the 1st intercostal space
CV-21 below the upper border of the sternum

Needling: 0.3 – 0.5 subcutaneous

Notes: CV-17 lies approximately midway between the nipples on males.

Uses: (i) CV-17 is the Front Mu point of the pericardium and is used to treat asthma, chest pain and palpitations. It is the *Influential point* of the respiratory system. (ii) CV-18 / 19 / 20 / 21 may be used for local chest pain and cough.

fig 170.

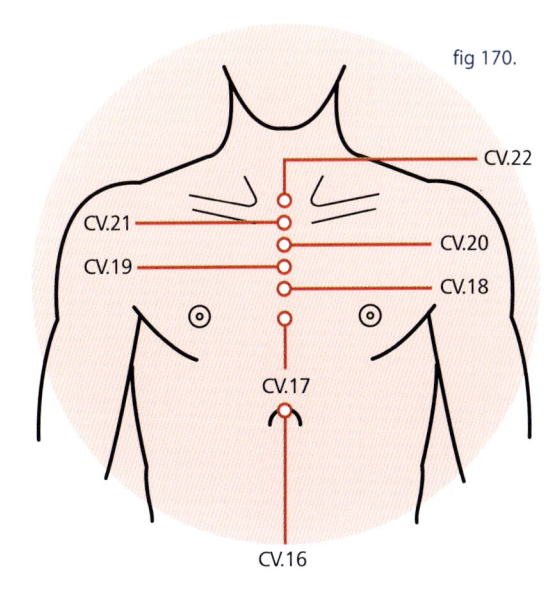

ACUPUNCTURE POINTS

CONCEPTION VESSEL 22

Location: In the centre of the suprasternal fossa (fig 171).

Needling: Perpendicular 0.2 cun

Note: This point lies 0.5 cun above the suprasternal notch.

Uses: Traditionally used for cough, wheezing and sore throat.

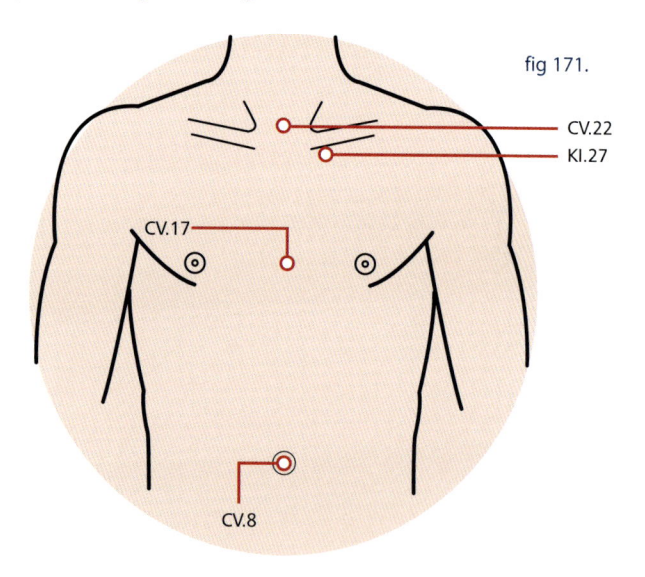

fig 171.

ACUPUNCTURE POINTS

CONCEPTION VESSEL 23
Location: On the midline of the neck in the depression above the hyoid bone (fig 172).

Needling: Oblique insertion 0.5 cun towards the base of the tongue

Note: To locate the Hyoid bone, palpate the Adam's apple and slide the finger upwards. Alternatively palpate the underside of the chin and slide the finger towards the throat until it rests in a shallow depression.

Uses: Traditionally used for loss of voice, especially after stroke.

fig 172.

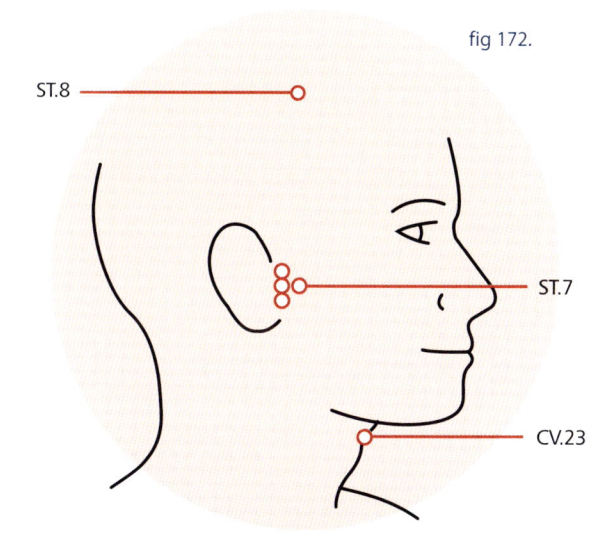

ACUPUNCTURE POINTS

CONCEPTION VESSEL 24

Location: Above the chin in the depression in the centre of the mentolabial groove (fig 173).

Needling: 0.3 cun perpendicular.

Uses: Traditionally used for facial paresis.

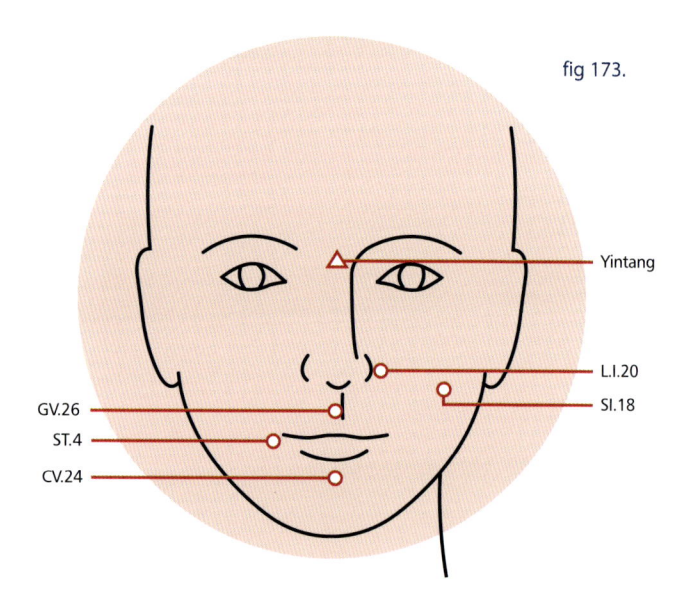

fig 173.

- Yintang
- L.I.20
- SI.18
- GV.26
- ST.4
- CV.24

ACUPUNCTURE POINTS

EXTRA POINTS

Upper Extremity

BAXIE (EX-UE 9)
Location: Four points between the metacarpal heads, proximal to the web margins (fig 174).

Needling: 0.5 – 0.8 cun oblique insertion along the shafts of the metacarpal bones.

Note: The points are more easily located and needled when a loose fist is formed.

Uses: Pain, stiffness, and numbness in the fingers and hand diseases.

SHIXUAN (EX-UE 11)
Location: On the tips of the fingers, 0.1 cun from the fingernail (fig 174).

Needling: Single prick only.

Uses: Traditionally used for loss of consciousness

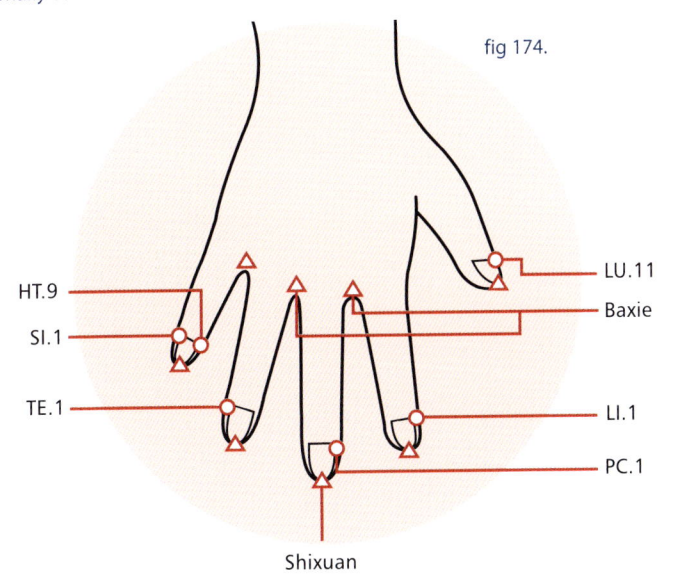

fig 174.

Shixuan

ACUPUNCTURE POINTS

SIFENG (EX-UE 10)

Location: On the palmar surface of the hand, at the midpoints of the transverse creases of the proximal interphalangeal joints of the fingers (fig 175).

Needling: Single prick only

Uses: Traditionally used in childhood digestive disorders and whooping cough.

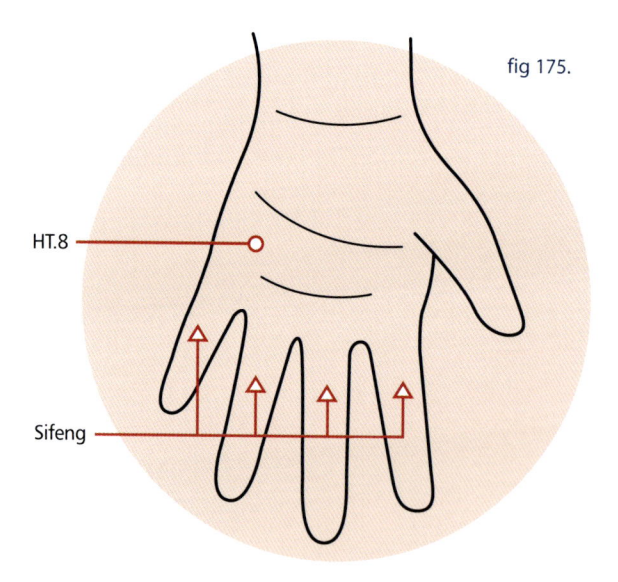

fig 175.

ACUPUNCTURE POINTS

LUOZHEN (EX-UE 8)

Location: On the back of the hand, in the depression between the 2nd and 3rd metacarpals, 0.5cun proximal to the metacarpophalangeal joint (fig 176).

Needling: 0.5 cun perpendicular

Note: This point is also named Wailaogong.

Uses: Stiff neck

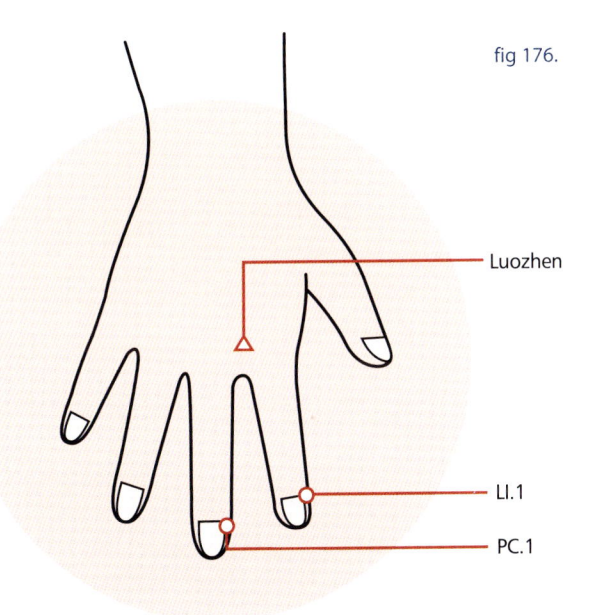

fig 176.

Luozhen

LI.1

PC.1

ACUPUNCTURE POINTS

JIANQIAN (EX-UE 48)

Location: Midway between LI-15 and the anterior axillary crease (fig 177).

Needling: 1.0 cun perpendicular

Uses: Local point for anterior shoulder pain.

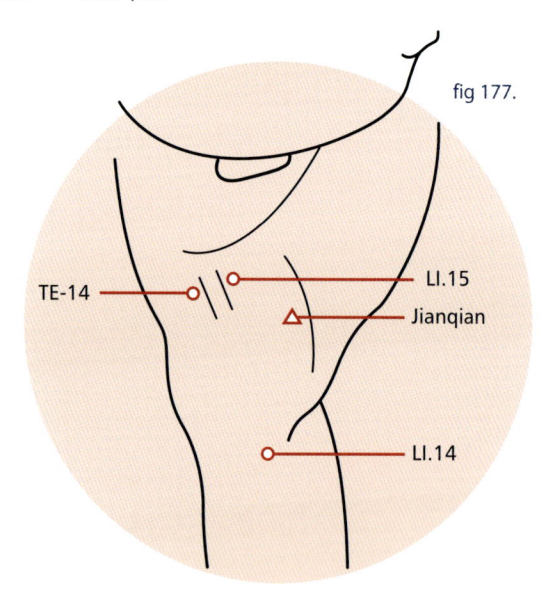

fig 177.

ACUPUNCTURE POINTS

ERBAI (EX-UE 2)

Location: 4 cun proximal to the transverse wrist crease (PC-7), either side of flexor carpi radialis (fig. 29).

Needling: 0.5 cun perpendicular

Uses: Haemorrhoids and anal itching.

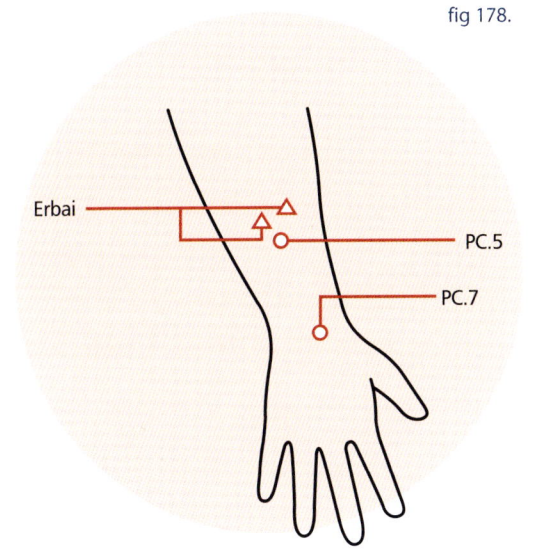

fig 178.

ACUPUNCTURE POINTS

YAOTONGXUE (EX-UE 7)

Location: On the back of the hand, between metacarpals 2 and 3 and 4 and 5 immediately distal to the metacarpal bases (fig 179).

Needling: 0.5 cun perpendicular

Uses: Acute lumbar pain.

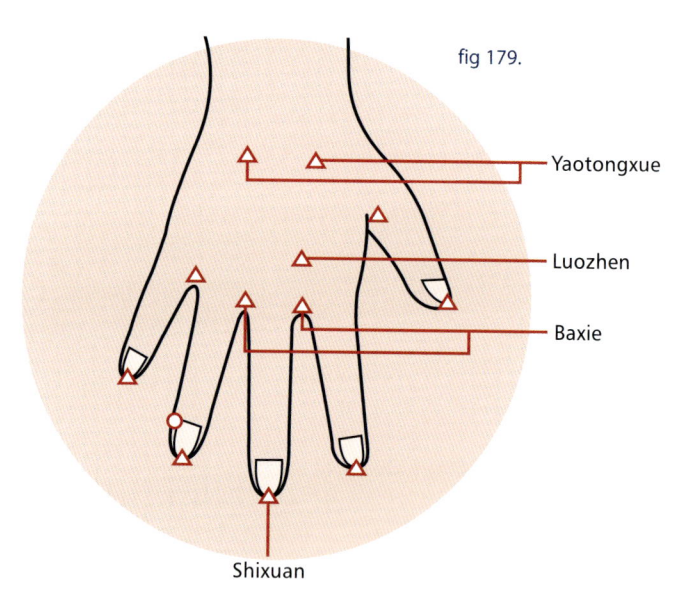

fig 179.
— Yaotongxue
— Luozhen
— Baxie
Shixuan

ACUPUNCTURE POINTS

Lower Extremity

BAFENG (EX-LE 10)

Location: On the dorsum of the foot, 0.5 cun proximal to the toe webs (fig 180).

Needling: Oblique insertion directed proximally 0.5 to 1 cun

Note: If the toes are crossed in the elderly, gently ease the metatarsal shafts apart as the needle is inserted.

Uses: Used to treat pain and dysfunction in the toes.

fig 180.

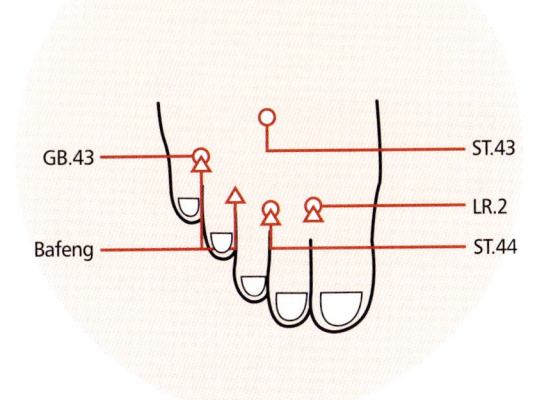

ACUPUNCTURE POINTS

LANWEIXUE (EX-LE 7)
Location: Approximately 2 cun distal to ST-36 (5 cun distal to ST-35, the lateral eye of the knee) on the right leg only (fig 181).

Needling: Perpendicular insertion 1 to 1.5 cun

Note: Locate at the point of maximum tenderness.

Uses: Traditionally used to treat pain from appendicitis. Claimed to be diagnostic in that tenderness is only seen when the appendix is inflamed.

DANNAGXUE (EX-LE 6)
Location: Between 1 and 2 cun distal to GB-34 on the right leg only (fig 181).

Needling: Perpendicular insertion 1 to 1.5 cun

Note: Locate at the point of maximum tenderness

Uses: Traditionally used to treat pain from cholecystitis

HEDING (EX-LE 2)
Location: In the depression in the middle of the superior border of the patella. (fig 181).

Needling: Perpendicular insertion 0.3 - 0.5 cun.

Uses: Patellofemoral pain of all types.

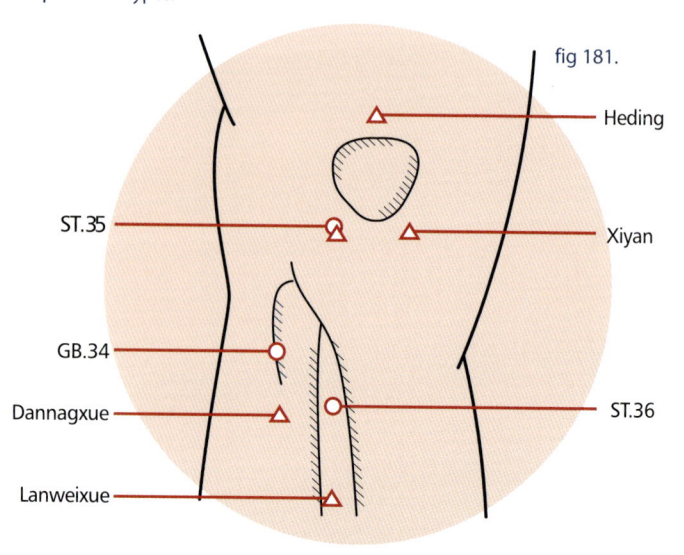

fig 181.

ACUPUNCTURE POINTS

XIYAN (EX-LE 5)

Location: With the knee flexed, two points either side of the patellar ligament (fig 181).

Needling: 0.5 – 1.0 cun towards the centre of the knee joint

Notes: These two points are also called the 'eyes' of the knee. The lateral point is ST-35.

Uses: Knee joint and patellar tendon pain.

Head and Neck

TAIYANG (EX-HN 5)

Location: At the temple in the depression 1 cun posterior to the midpoint between the lateral corner of the eyebrow and the outer canthus of the eye (fig 182).

Needling: Perpendicular needling 0.5 to 0.8 cun.

Uses: One sided headache, trigeminal neuralgia, facial paralysis.

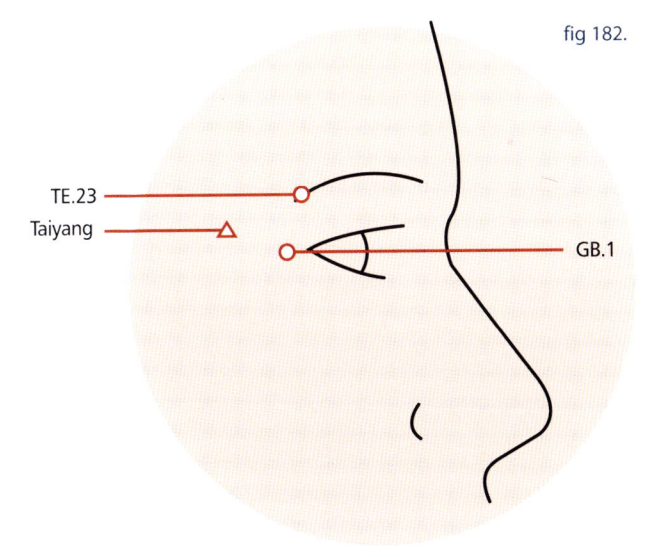

fig 182.

TE.23
Taiyang
GB.1

ACUPUNCTURE POINTS

YUYAO (EX-HN 4)

Location: In the centre of the eyebrow, directly above the pupil with the patient looking straight ahead (fig 183).

Needling: 0.3 - 0.5 cun subcutaneous.

Uses: Eye disorders, drooping eyelid.

fig 183.

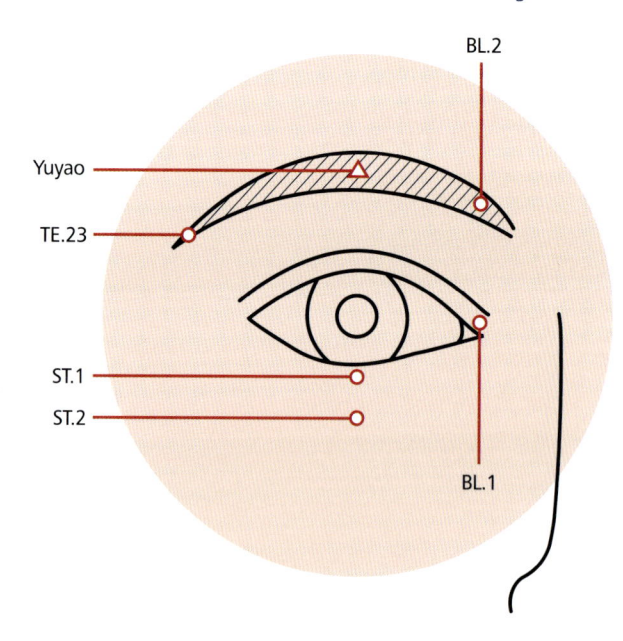

ACUPUNCTURE POINTS

YINTANG (EX-HN 3)

Location: On the midline of the forehead, between the eyebrows (fig 184).

Needling: 0.3 – 0.5 cun subcutaneous

Uses: Frontal headache, eye disease, blocked nose.

BITONG (EX-HN 8)

Location: Highest point of the nasolabial groove, at the junction between the nasal bone and cartilage (fig 184).

Note: This point is also called Shangyingxiang.

Needling: 0.3 – 0.5 cun cranial and medial

Uses: Blocked nose.

fig 184.

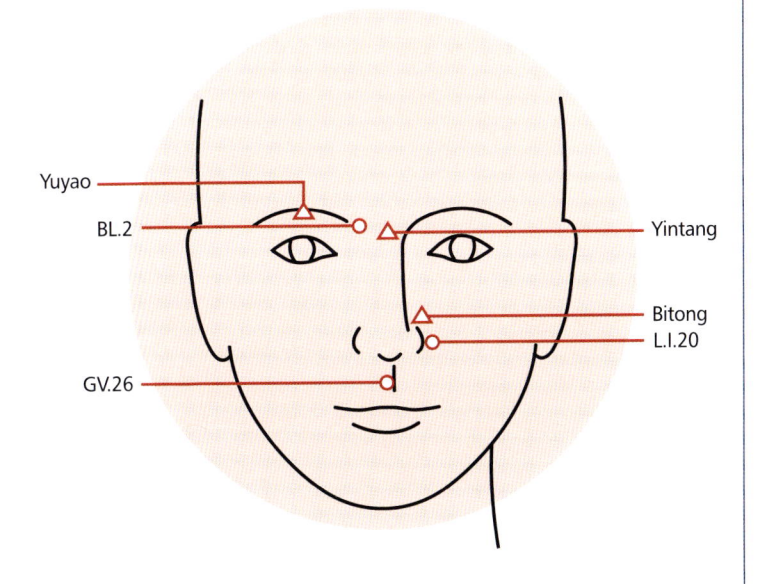

ACUPUNCTURE POINTS

YIMING (EX-HN 14)

Location: Behind the ear, 1 cun posterior to TE-17 (fig 185).

Needling: 0.5 cun perpendicular

Uses: Traditionally used to treat diseases of the eye and tinnitus.

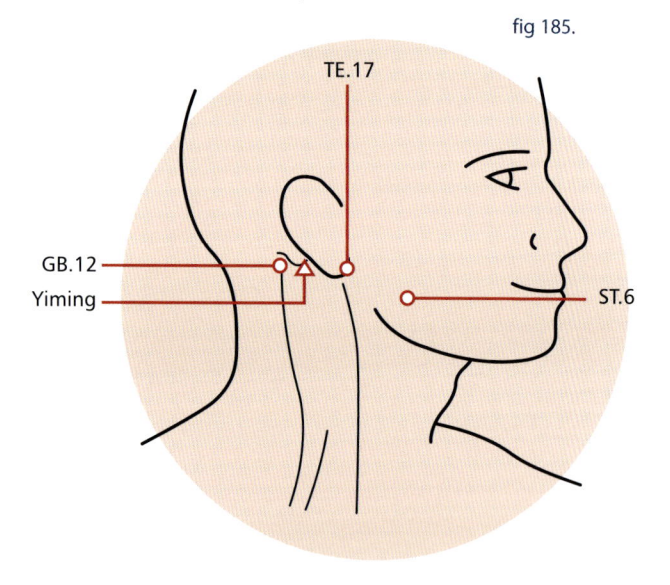

fig 185.

ACUPUNCTURE POINTS

SISCHENCONG (EX-HN 1)

Location: At the vertex of the head. Four points each lying 1 cun from GV-20 anterior, posterior and lateral (fig 186).

Needling: Transverse insertion 0.5 - 1.0 cun towards GV-20.

Uses: Traditionally used to *calm the spirit* and *pacify wind* in the case of headaches.

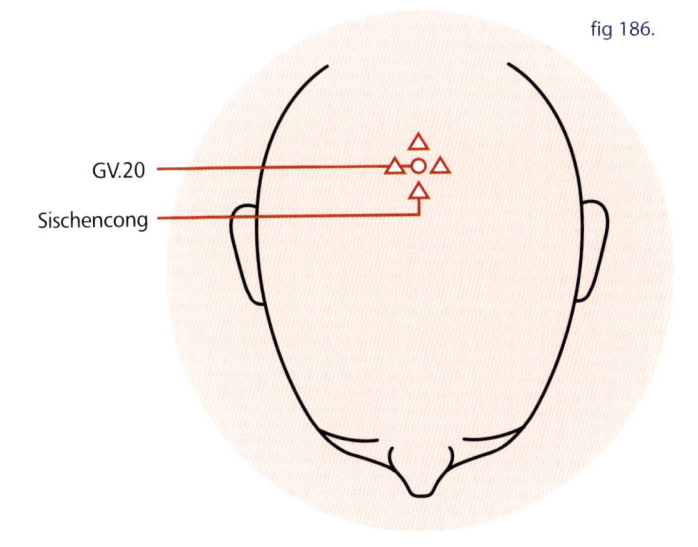

fig 186.

GV.20
Sischencong

ACUPUNCTURE POINTS

Back

DINGCHUAN (EX-B1)

Location: 0.5 cun lateral to the depression below the spinous process of C7, level with GV-14 (fig 187).

Needling: Perpendicular insertion 0.5 to 0.8 cun.

Uses: Cough and asthma

SHIQIZHUIXIA (EX-B8)

Location: On the low back, in the depression below the spinous process of L5 (fig. 188).

Needling: 1.5 cun oblique cranially.

Uses: Lumbo-sacral pain, menstrual disorders.

HUATUOJIAJI (EX-B2)

Location: 0.5 cun lateral to the depressions below the spinous processes from T1 to L5 (fig 187 & 188).

Needling: Oblique insertion towards the spine 0.5 to 1 cun.

Uses: Local midline spinal pain, or segmentally to treat the internal organs.

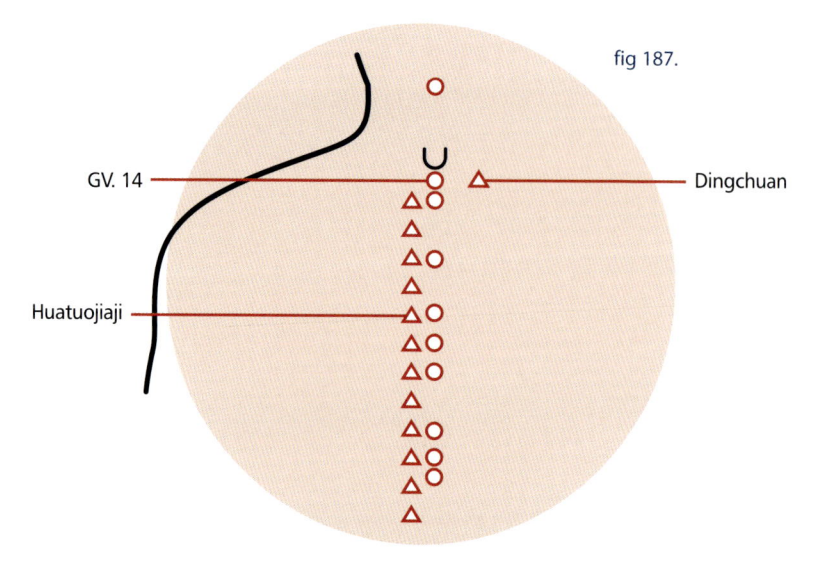

fig 187.

GV. 14

Dingchuan

Huatuojiaji

ACUPUNCTURE POINTS

YAOQI (EX-B9)

Location: 2 cun proximal to the tip of the coccyx (fig 188).

Needling: 1.5 cun oblique cranially.

Uses: Headache, constipation, epilepsy.

YAOYAN (EX-B7)

Location: 3.5 cun lateral to the midline, level with the lower border of L4 (fig 188).

Needling: 1.0 cun perpendicular

Note: These points are also called the lumbar 'eyes'

Uses: Local point for lumbar pain.

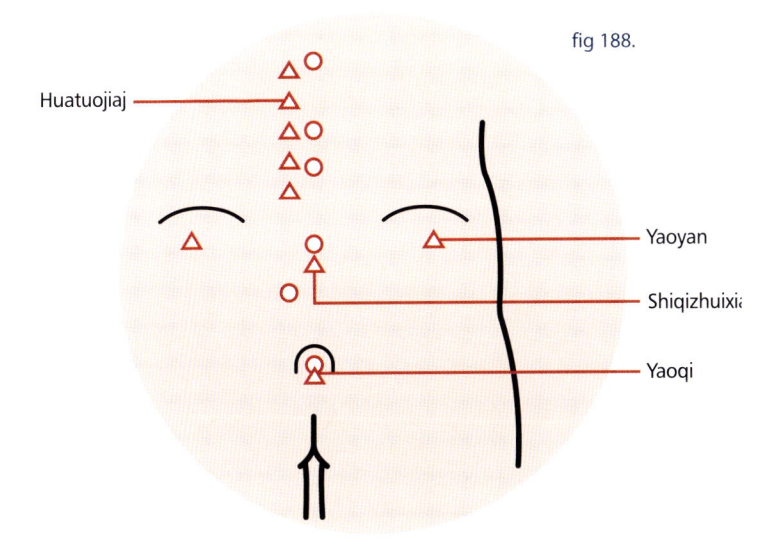

fig 188.

Huatuojiaji

Yaoyan

Shiqizhuixia

Yaoqi

EXTRA

REFERENCES AND SOURCE MATERIAL.

References and source material.

Deadman, P., Al-Khafaji, M., and Baker, K (1998) A Manual of acupuncture.
Journal of Chinese Medicine Publications. Hove, UK.

Focks, C (2008) Atlas of acupuncture. Churchill Livingstone. Oxford, UK.

Hecker, HU, Steveling, A., Peuker, E., Kastner, J., and Liebchen, K (2001)
Colour atlas of acupuncture. Thieme. New York.

Lander, D (2006) The Jing Luo. The College of Traditional Acupuncture. Warwick. UK

Lian, Y-L., Chen, C-Y, Hammes, M., and Kolster, BC (1999)
The Seirin pictorial atlas of acupuncture.

Norris, CM (2001) Acupuncture: treatment of musculoskeletal conditions.
Butterworth Heinemann. Oxford.

Qpuncture. CD Rom program. Qpuncture Inc. Anaheim, California. USA

Xinnong, C (1999) Chinese acupuncture and moxibustion. (revised edition).
Foreign languages press. Beijing.

Zhenguo, Y (2003) Anatomical atlas of acupuncture points: a photo location guide.
Donica Publishing. UK

APPENDIX

APPENDIX

Types of acupuncture point

When treating musculoskeletal conditions, acupuncture points may be selected as:
- Local – those which are painful to palpation (traditionally called 'ahshi points, these are often also trigger points). And those within the local painful area.
- Distal points – are those along the meridians which pass through the painful area.
- General points are those which have specific functions which may or may not be related to pain.

A number of acupuncture points have specific functions as follows:

Source (Qi) points
Said to be where the Qi is housed. The source points of the yang meridians (outer face of limb) are used to regulate the whole meridian. Those of the yin meridians (inner face of the limb) regulate the meridians and also the corresponding organ.

Source points

Lung	LU-9	Bladder	BL-64
Large intestine	LI-4	Kidney	KI-3
Stomach	ST-42	Pericardium	PC-7
Spleen	SP-3	Triple Energiser	TE-4
Heart	HT-7	Gall bladder	GB-40
Small intestine	SI-4	Liver	LR-3

The five shu points
The five shu (transporting) points are all located distal to the elbow or knee. They are traditionally viewed as a strengthening of the Qi flow from the end of the meridian into the body, analogous to water flowing from well to spring, stream, river and finally the sea. Clinically the points are used as follows:

- **Well** – acute conditions / restores consciousness
- **Spring** – deficiency (empty) heat in febrile diseases, especially the upper portions of channels. More commonly used in yang channels
- **Stream** – Often used to treat Chronic obstructive syndrome (Bi Syndrome) with invasion of pathogenic damp showing as pain and heaviness in the joints especially. The Shu stream points correspond to the source points in yin channels.
- **River** – commonly used for cough / dyspnoea. Some of the Shu river points have important actions on musculoskeletal conditions
- **Sea** – commonly used for counterflow Qi having a strong influence on the stomach and intestines.

In addition to the classic shu points, three meridians have lower he-sea points on the leg ST-37 (large intestine), ST-39 (small intestine) and BL-39 (triple energiser).

POINT CLASSIFICATION

Shu points

	Well	Spring	Stream	River	Sea
Lung	LU-11	LU-10	LU-9	LU-9	LU-5
Spleen	SP-1	SP-2	SP-3	SP-4	SP-5
Heart	HT-9	HT-8	HT-7	HT-4	HT-3
Kidney	KI-1	KI-2	KI-3	KI-7	KI-10
Pericardium	PC-9	PC-8	PC-7	PC-5	PC-3
Liver	LR-1	LR-2	LR-3	LR-4	LR-8
Large Intestine	LI-1	LI-2	LI-3	LI-5	LI-11
Stomach	ST-45	ST-44	ST-43	ST-41	ST-36
Small Intestine	SI-1	SI-2	SI-3	SI-5	SI-8
Bladder	BL-67	BL-66	BL-65	BL-60	BL-40
Triple Energiser	TE-1	TE-2	TE-3	TE-6	TE-10
Gall Bladder	GB-44	GB-43	GB-41	GB-38	GB-34

Tonification (mother) points and Sedation (child) points

The tonification point is used to increase the energy in a meridian, the sedation point to reduce it. Sedation points are used in cases of excess energy within a meridian (hot, acute conditions) while tonification points are used in cases of underactivity in the meridian (cold, chronic).

Tonification and Sedation points

Meridian	Tonification point	Sedation point
Lung	LU-9	LU-5
Large intestine	LI-11	LI-2
Stomach	ST-41	ST-45
Spleen	SP-2	SP-5
Heart	HT-9	HT-7
Small intestine	SI-3	SI-8
Bladder	BL-67	BL-65
Kidney	KI-7	KI-1
Pericardium	PC-9	PC-7
Triple Energiser	TE-3	TE-10
Gall Bladder	GB-43	GB-38
Liver	LR-8	LR-2

POINT CLASSIFICATION

XI (CLEFT) POINTS
Used to treat acute disorders of the corresponding organ.

Xi-cleft points

Lung	LU-6	Bladder	BL-63
Large intestine	LI-7	Kidney	KI-5
Stomach	ST-34	Pericardium	PC-4
Spleen	SP-8	Triple Energiser	TE-7
Heart	HT-6	Gall Bladder	GB-36
Small intestine	SI-6	Liver	LR-6

Luo (connecting) points
The 12 meridians are grouped in pairs, each of the pair being either yin (inner face of limb) or yang (outer face of limb). The Luo point is the point at which coupled channels link.

Luo-connecting points

Lung	LU-7	Bladder	BL-58
Large intestine	LI-6	Kidney	KI-4
Stomach	ST-40	Pericardium	PC-6
Spleen	SP-4	Triple Energiser	TE-5
Heart	HT-5	Gall Bladder	GB-37
Small intestine	SI-7	Liver	LR-5

POINT CLASSIFICATION

Confluence (tuning) points

In addition to the 12 standard meridians, there are 8 extra (extraordinary) meridians, as follows:

- *Governing vessel* travelling along the posterior midline.
- *Conception vessel* on the anterior midline.
- *Penetrating vessel* linking with the Kidney and Stomach channels
- *Girdle vessel* travelling around the waist
- *Yang heel (motility) vessel* running on the lateral aspect of the body
- *Yin heel (motility) vessel* on the medial aspect of the leg
- *Yang linking vessel* ascending with the Gall Bladder channel
- *Yin linking vessel* On the medial aspect of the leg sharing points with the Spleen channel

These extraordinary meridians join the standard meridians at the confluence points, and are normally activated in pairs.

Confluence points

Extra meridian	Confluence points	Used for symptoms affecting:
Penetrating/Yin linking	SP-4/PC-6	Heart, circulation and gut.
Girdling/Yang linking	GB-41/TE-5	Lateral side of body, low back
Du/Yang motility	SI-3/BL-62	Head, neck, back and CNS
Ren/Yin motility	LU-7/KI-6	Throat, lungs, organs, & gynaecological,

Influential (master) points

The 8 influential points are especially useful when treating elderly or weak patients. Each point corresponds to a separate system or tissue.

Influential points

Tissue and organ affected	Influential points
Zang organs	LR-13
Fu organs	CV-12
Respiratory system	CV-17
Blood	BL-17
Bone	BL-11
Bone marrow	GB-39
Muscle and tendon	GB-34
Vascular system	LU-9

POINT CLASSIFICATION

Front mu (gathering) and back shu (transporting) points

The 12 mu (anterior) and 12 shu (posterior) points are used in the diagnosis and treatment of conditions affecting the body organs. The back shu points all lie along the inner bladder (BL) channel and have segmental relation to the viscera.

Front mu and back shu points

Zang Fu organ	Back shu points	Front mu points
Lung	BL-13	LU-1
Large intestine	BL-25	ST-25
Stomach	BL-21	CV-12
Spleen	BL-20	LR-13
Heart	BL-15	CV-14
Small intestine	BL-27	CV-4
Bladder	BL-28	CV-3
Kidney	BL-23	GB-25
Pericardium	BL-14	CV-17
Triple Energiser	BL-22	CV-5
Gall Bladder	BL-19	GB-24
Liver	BL-18	LR-14

Heavenly star points and command points.

These two groups of points are used extensively in the treatment of musculoskeletal conditions. They are used to supplement the effect of local and distal points.

Heavenly star points and their use in musculoskeletal conditions.

LU-7	Headache, especially when one-sided
LI-4	Headache and facial pain
LI-11	Elbow pain
ST-36	Stomach pain, knee pain
ST-44	Chills in the hands and feet
HT-5	Heaviness of the body
BL-40	Lumbar pain radiating to the knee
BL-57	Lumbar pain radiating to the calf
BL-60	Lumbar pain radiating to the foot
GB-39	Painful obstruction syndrome (fixed bi)
GB-34	Painful obstruction syndrome (cold bi)
LR-3	Painful obstruction syndrome (fixed bi)

POINT CLASSIFICATION

Command points and their use in musculoskeletal treatments.

ST-36	Abdomen
BL-40	Lumbar region
LU-7	Head and nape of neck
LI-4	Face and mouth
PC-6	Chest and lateral costal area
GV-26	Resuscitation (digital pressure only)

Window of Heaven points

Traditionally used to treat imbalance between the body and head where *Qi or blood rushes upwards.* Used clinically to treat emotional and psychological disturbances. Also sometimes used for swelling / nodules on the throat and neck

LU-3	CV-22
ST-9	SI-16
LI-18	SI-17
TE-16	GV-16
BL-10	PC-1

NOTES

INDEX

A
Abdominal distension	34
Achilles pain	102
Achilles tendon	94, 95, 101
Amenorrhea	36
Anal diseases	168
Anatomical snuffbox	15
Angina	109
Ankle joint	44
Appendix	181
Asthma	187

B
Biceps tendinopathy	7
Biceps tendon	89, 90
Bleeding	48
Blocked nose	184
Blurred vision	69
Brachial artery	60
Breathlessness	9

C
Carotid artery	123
Carpal tunnel disorder	111
Carotid artery	29
CVA	163
Cheek	26
Chest conditions	7
Chest pain	108
Cholecystitis	181
Coccygeal pain	87, 160
Congestion	24
Constipation	35, 188
Costal region	140
Cough	8, 30, 32, 34, 170
Cubital crease	6
Cun	4

D
Deltoid muscle	19
Delto-pectoral triangle	6
De-Quervain's syndrome	9
Diarrhea	35
Dizziness	6, 100
Dorsalis pedis artery	44
Drooping eye lid	136, 183
Dysmenorrhea	52, 168
Dyspnea	34, 105

E
Ear	13, 74
Extensor carpi radialis	16
Eye	77, 99
Eyelid	128
Eyesight	25, 77

F
Face	14, 46
Facial pain	26
Facial paralysis	24, 25, 173, 182
Fainting	167
Femoral pulse	55
Fixed bi syndrome	146
Frontal headache	78
Foetus malposition	99

G
Genitals	157
Gynecological disorders	153

H
Hemorrhoids	178
Hamstring	88
Hand diseases	174
Headache	79, 132
Heel pain	96
Hemiplegia	143
Hiccups	30
Hip pain	38
Hypo chondric pain	159

I
Impotence	103
Infertility	36
Insomnia	6, 63
Intercostal neuralgia	57, 117
Intestinal disorders	42

L
Lateral pterygoid	28

ACUPUNCTURE POCKETBOOK

INDEX

M
Malposition of foetus	99
Masseter muscle	27, 66
Mastitis	66
Menstruation	51, 103
Mouth	12, 14

N
Nasal passages	23
Nausea	110
Night sweats	162
Nose	13, 24
Nosebleeds	23

O
Occipital headache	80
Oedema	45

P
Palpitations	65, 109
Patellar tendon	41
Peritoneal cavity	56
Phalanx	4, 21
Piriformis syndrome	92
Plantar fascial pain	100
Pneumothorax	20, 73, 122
Popliteal artery	90
Pregnancy	36
Prolapse of uterus	154

Q
Quadriceps	38, 39

R
Radial artery	9
Radial styloid	8

S
Salivary gland	27
Skin disorders	17
Sternocleidomastoid	21, 22, 29
Stomach	41
Stomach pain	40
Subclavian artery	5
Subclavicular fossa	5

Supracondylar ridge	17
Supraspinatus	20
Symphysis pubis	55

T
Teeth	26, 27, 46
Temporal headache	147
Temporalis	28
Tennis elbow	17
Testis	43
Thenar eminence	10
Throat	13, 21, 74
Throat and mouth	12
Throat disorders	102
Tibialis Anterior	41
Tinnitus	15, 124, 125, 127, 148
TMJ	28
Toe pain	98
Tooth conditions	15
Toothache	27
Trapezius muscles	138
Trigeminal neuralgia	75
Tubercle of Navicular	50
Twitching	26

U
Urination	54
Uterus	85

V
Vertigo	165
Voice	74

W
Wheezing	8, 32, 106, 171
Whooping cough	175
Wrist pain	10

Z
Zygomatic arch	28

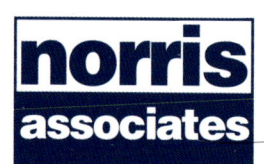

norris associates
BOOKS BY CHRIS NORRIS

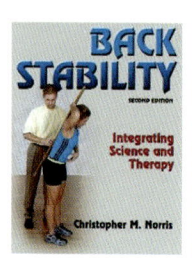

BACK STABILITY (2nd Edition)
Presenting an integrated approach to back rehabilitation this updated and extended book covers

Biomechanics / Stabilisation Mechanisms/ Posture / Muscle Imbalance / Abdominal Training / Establishing Stability / Advanced Training / Building a Program / Preventing Reinjury. Exercises are presented with teaching points and clinical guidelines.

2008, 347 pages, B & W photos throughout, 160 Exercises. Hardback. Human Kinetics.

£27.50

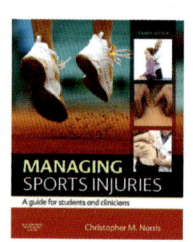

MANAGING SPORTS INJURIES (4th edition)
Now in its fourth edition with the revised title - Managing Sports Injuries: a guide for students and clinicians - this highly practical guide maintains its evidence-based approach while introducing new material from both research and clinical sources. It is a comprehensive resource for the management of soft-tissue injuries, focusing on therapy.

Tissue healing/Sports massage/taping/exercise therapy/sports first aid/gait/lower limb/ upper limb/ trunk/

2011, Hardback. 432 pages 215 colour figures, 590 colour photographs

£47.99

COMPLETE GUIDE TO ABDOMINAL TRAINING (2nd Edition)
This best selling book has become the definitive guide to safe and effective development of the trunk muscles

How the Spine Works / Concepts of Abdominal Training /Posture / Diet / Trunk Exercise Dangers / Foundation Movements Exercise Progression / AbTraining Sport and Water / Abdominal Muscle Research / Developing Programmes.

2009, 232 pages, Over 250 colour photographs and illustrations. Paperback. A&C Black.

£18.99

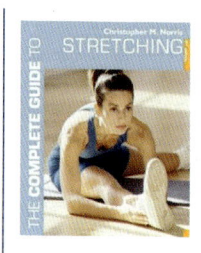

COMPLETE GUIDE TO STRETCHING (3rd Edition)
A clearly illustrated guide to stretching backed by biomechanics and research. This new edition of 'Stretching' has over 160 exercises and new sections on yoga stretches and fascial stretching.

Stretching Biomechanics / Joint Structure / Training Principles / Posture. Stretching the Nerves/ Fascial Stretching / Partner Stretching / Dynamic Stretching / Research / Sports Injuries / Sport Specifics/ Measuring flexibility.

2007, Softback 247 pages. Full illustrations throughout. A&C Black.

£15.99

BUY ONLINE:
www.norrisassociates.co.uk
16 Lawton Street, Congleton, Cheshire CW12 1RP   T: 01260 290564   E: info@norrisassociates.co.uk